JAPAN ENCOUNTERED

A Brief (and Highly-Selective)
Survey of Famous Westerners
in the Land of the
Rising Sun

App - 1
B+ 58
=
App =

Scott Wright

C h
13 - 16

ch. 9

D1527055

University Press of America, Inc.
Lanham • New York • London

Copyright © 1996 by
University Press of America,® Inc.
4720 Boston Way
Lanham, Maryland 20706

3 Henrietta Street
London, WC2E 8LU England

Library of Congress Cataloging-in-Publication Data

Wright, Scott
Japan encountered : a brief (and highly-selective) survey of famous
Westerners in the land of the Rising Sun / Scott Wright.
p.   cm.
1. Aliens--Japan--Biography. 2. Japan--Officials and employees,
Alien--Biography. 3. Japan--Civilization--Western influences.   I.
Title.
DS832.7.AlW75   1996   952 --dc20   96-24526   CIP

ISBN 0-7618-0427-7 (cloth: alk. ppr.)
ISBN 0-7618-0428-5 (pbk: alk. ppr.)

TO
John and Kay
and Rick and Kinuko

Contents

*   *   *

Illustrations

Acknowledgements

The author hereby acknowledges and is grateful for permission to quote from the following previously copyrighted material:

The Frank Lloyd Wright Foundation for brief quotations from Frank Lloyd Wright's *An Autobiography* (1932 edition) (Chapter 9).

Random House, Inc. for brief quotations from the Waley and Seidensticker translations of *The Tale of Genji* (Chapter 10); the works of James Michener (Chapter 14 and Appendix III); and Michael Crichton's *Rising Sun* (Appendix III).

Quotations from *The Dharma Bums* by Jack Kerouac (Chapter 14). Copyright © 1958 by Jack Kerouac, © renewed 1986 by Stella Kerouac and Jan Kerouac. Used by permission of Viking Penguin, a division of Penguin Books USA Inc.

Quoted material in Appendix III reprinted with the permission of Simon & Schuster from *Dragon* by Clive Cussler. Copyright © 1990 by Clive Cussler Enterprises, Inc.

Introduction

The chief purpose of this volume, as the title suggests, is to provide a brief and highly-selective survey of famous Westerners in Japan. In the process of selection I have sought individuals who it seemed to me were representative of various 'types' of Westerners who have been involved with the country, running the gamut from missionaries to diplomats, and including as well soldiers, artists of various sorts, travelers, athletes, and general cultural observers. It is my hope that through the encounter of this broad spectrum of individuals, representing different historical periods as well as widely divergent occupations and outlooks, modern students of Japan in the West will be able to gain a sense of the attractions, points of conflict, and considerable range of meanings that Japan has had for Westerners over the years. In a broader sense, too, at a time when the need for an understanding of other cultures has taken on a new significance and importance in college and university curriculums, it is hoped that this method of observing the interaction of Westerners with another, essentially non-Western culture will serve as a tool for the fostering of broader cultural understanding.

Since the book is planned primarily for use as a supplementary text in what often constitutes the second half of a Japanese history survey, each chapter ends with a series of questions for study and classroom discussion. The list of sources at the end of the volume and the various items cited in the footnotes accompanying each chapter can be consulted for further material on the individuals included. The essays which comprise this work make no attempt at completeness of biographical coverage, but seek rather to explore in as direct a manner as possible the specific character of each individual's relationship with Japan. For readers desiring further background on Japan's contact with

Introduction

the West prior to World War II, the author's "The Decision to Attack Pearl Harbor: A Long-term View," included in the appendix, can be used. Finally, it should be noted that the decision to deal solely with famous "Westerners" in Japan implies no denial of, or failure to recognize, the equally significant and interesting story of individuals from other, *non*-Western backgrounds, be they Chinese, Korean, African, etc., in the country.

*   *   *

As is customary in any work of this type the author has many people whom he wishes to thank for help and support during the writing of it. Among the most important are: John and Kathryn Hodge, Richard and Kinuko Jambor, and V. Dixon Morris for their friendship and many insights into Japanese language and culture; Ms. Inoue of the Library Staff at Osaka Gakuin University for much patience and assistance; the brothers and community of the Marist Brothers International School in Suma for spiritual guidance and support; my wife, Betty, and son, Adam, who lived with me in Japan during the writing of it and offered help on many levels; and the University of St. Thomas which granted me the leave of absence and sabbatical which provided the time for writing it. Special thanks goes also to Jan Amundson for her tireless help and assistance in doing the computer layout for this work.

Scott Wright
St. Paul, Minnesota
January, 1996

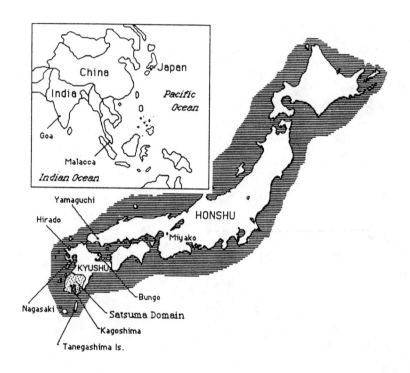

China

India

Japan

Pacific
Ocean

Goa

Malacca

Indian Ocean

Yamaguchi

Hirado

HONSHU

Miyako

KYUSHU

Bungo

Nagasaki

Satsuma Domain

Kagoshima

Tanegashima Is.

Chapter 1

Saint Francis Xavier
(1506-1552)

Architect of Japan's Christian Century

One of the most successful missionaries in the modern history of the Roman Catholic Church, Saint Francis Xavier played a key role in the introduction of Christianity into Japan in the 16th century. Born in Navarre in northern Spain in 1506, he was the third son of a nobleman influential at the court of the King of Navarre, but because of his birth order was designated for a clerical rather than a political career. He went to Paris in 1525 to begin his theological studies and in 1529 met Ignatius Loyola and was active with him in the series of events leading to the founding of the Society of Jesus (or Jesuit Order) which was officially recognized by the Church in 1540. Xavier was ordained a priest in 1537. His original intention (as well as that of the others of the group involved in the founding of the new order) was to undertake a pilgrimage to the Holy Land to work for the conversion of unbelievers, but in the late 1530's and early 1540's the group came under the influence of King John III of Portugal who was seeking priests to bring Christianity to the new lands which Portugal was in the process of discovering in Asia. When one of the team of individuals originally chosen by Ignatius to go to this region became ill, Xavier replaced him. He left Rome in the spring of 1540, and, after spending a brief period in Lisbon, arrived at Goa on the western coast of India in May of 1542.

For the next several years the new missionary ministered to the poor fishermen and pearl hunters living on the southeastern coast of India, many of whom (perhaps as many as 20,000) had accepted the Christian religion earlier for political reasons but had had little opportunity for spiritual nuturing. He also extended the influence of Christianity in the region, converting 10,000 Macuans from the southwestern part of India to the faith in 1544. From India, in 1545, he traveled to the Portuguese colony of Malacca on the tip of the Malaysian peninsula, and it was there, after meeting a Japanese named Anjiro who was interested in Christianity, that Xavier first learned of the Japanese people and began to develop his great interest in them.[1]

After doing further missionary work in Malaysia and the Spice Islands-- and a return trip to India in 1548-9-- Xavier set sail for Japan, arriving at Kagoshima at the southern end of Kyushu on the fifteenth of August, 1549. Japan's first contact with Europeans had occurred only six years earlier, in 1543, when a small party of Portuguese fishermen had been shipwrecked on the island of Tanegashima south of Kyushu, and Xavier and his tiny party thus constituted a considerable novelty for the local inhabitants. For his part, Xavier was greatly impressed with the individuals he encountered, writing in his first (and often-quoted) letter from Japan that the Japanese were "the best people yet discovered."[2] With Anjiro acting as interpreter, he was successful in meeting with the local *daimyo* (or political leader)-- Shimazu Takahisa, lord of Satsuma-- who welcomed him warmly.[3] Xavier, having learned of the existence of an emperor who resided in Miyako (Kyoto), also asked to see this individual, a request which Takahisa agreed to but never followed through on. In the meantime, once again with Anjiro's

---

[1] Information concerning Japan apparently abounded in this region, since Xavier also states in a letter written in 1549 that: "About the month of April, 1547, I fell in with a Portuguese merchant, a man of exceeding piety and veracity, who talked to me of Japan, lately discovered." Xavier's great interest in the new area is reflected in what follows when he writes: "It seems that the Christian religion might prosper better there than in any other region of the Indies, since the people are of inquiring minds eager for enlightenment beyond any upon earth." (From Harold S. Williams, *Foreigners in Mikadoland* (Tokyo: Tuttle, 1963), p. 19.)

[2] *The New Encyclopaedia Britannica* (Chicago: University of Chicago, 1990), vol. 12, p. 794.

[3] Xavier's arrival in Japan had occurred at a propitious time in Japanese history, since the political turmoil of the period made many of the local leaders throughout the country eager to court the power and influence of the foreigners.

assistance, Xavier began efforts to convert the local inhabitants. A brief summary of the Christian doctrines was translated into Japanese, and during the ten months that he remained in Satsuma approximately 150 individuals were brought to the faith. Observing the wealth and cultural sophistication of the *daimyo* and other local officials, Xavier turned away from the model of poverty which he had followed among the poor people of India and Malaysia and adopted a somewhat more formal and on occasion even regal style. He also made contact with the leaders of the local Buddhist sects and entered into dialogue with them on the nature of their religious beliefs, receiving a polite but largely disinterested reaction to his own presentation of Christian doctrine. Negative reaction to his verbal attacks on various local customs, coupled with the realization that Takahisa was not going to take him to see the emperor, led him to travel to the port of Hirado in the northwestern part of Kyushu in 1550.

At Hirado, too, he was well-received by the local *daimyo*, and after leaving one of his associates behind to administer to the people of that region, he proceeded westward to Yamaguchi at the western end of Honshu. At Yamaguchi he was successful in meeting with Ouchi Yoshitaka, one of the most powerful regional leaders in Japan at that time, but managed to offend him by reading a tract on the Christian religion which included an attack on homosexual practices-- common among the warrior class of Japan in those days-- and for a brief period the party feared for their lives. The preaching of similar moralisms among the people of the region met with a similar result, and just before Christmas the same year Xavier left Yamaguchi, determined now to go to Miyako to meet with the emperor.

He arrived in Miyako, after a difficult overland journey, but was unable to see either the *shogun* (the country's military leader) or the emperor. (The former had left the city, and the latter, who possessed no real power in Japan at this time, was living, unbeknown to the missionary, in obscurity in an old palace.) He then returned to Yamaguchi where a second meeting with the powerful Lord Ouchi went better than the first, and he was able to convince several Buddhist monks who were present of the basic similarities between the Christian and Buddhist religions. Subsequent preaching and discourse, however, convinced Xavier of the basic incompatibility of the two faiths, and tensions with the local inhabitants again surfaced. Following these largely unsuccessful efforts, Xavier received an invitation from the *daimyo* of Bungo in Kyushu to come to that domain.[4] It was there that

---

[4]This individual's motives, despite his later conversion to the faith, seem to

he had his greatest successes as a missionary in Japan, converting many Japanese to the faith, including Otomo Sorin, the local *daimyo*, himself. In late 1551, leaving others in charge of the five communities and approximately 2,000 converts he had made during his slightly more than two years in the country, Xavier left Japan to return to Gao. After a brief time there attending to administrative details he embarked on a trip to China, having come to the conclusion that that country, which had been so important in the cultural development of Japan, also offered a rich ground for missionary effort. On December 3, 1552, however, while waiting on a small island off the coast of China for permission to enter the country, he died of a fever.

Although Xavier's arrival represents what historian G.B. Sansom refers to as merely "[t]he first phase of missionary endeavor in Japan,"[5] his experience is important to any understanding of the later history of that subject. Following Xavier, a period sometimes referred to as "the Christian century in Japan"[6] ensued. Portuguese, and later Spanish, missionaries were sent to the country, schools, hospitals and seminaries were founded, and by the beginning of the 17th century perhaps as many as 300,000 Japanese had converted to the faith, chiefly on Kyushu and the western end of Honshu. Nagasaki, on the western side of Kyushu, became an important Christian center. Like Xavier, however, these later missionaries often failed to separate the nonessential European trappings of the faith from its essential doctrinal core, requiring believers to give up too many of their native customs and traditions as a prerequisite for conversion. Like Xavier too, they failed to fully appreciate the underlying political conditions of this time in Japanese history-- the period when Oda Nobunaga, Toyotomi Hideyoshi and Tokugawa Ieyasu were in the process of unifying the country-- conditions which often served to motivate the leaders of the day to either accept or reject the new religion quite independently of spiritual considerations. Finally, in ways unforeseen by Xavier, the effects of the Protestant Reformation in Europe, which brought individuals from other, non-Catholic countries (most notably the Netherlands and England) to Japan in the early years of the 17th century (and the ensuing strife between the representatives of these countries-- see next chapter), also undercut the efforts of missionaries to continue

---

have been as much economic as spiritual (see G.B. Sansom, *A History of Japan, 1334-1615* (Tokyo: Tuttle, 1974), p. 264).

[5] *The Western World and Japan: A study in the Interaction of European and Asiatic Cultures* (Tokyo, Tuttle, 1977), p. 122.

[6] See, for example, C.R. Boxer, *The Christian Century In Japan, 1549-1650* (Berkeley, CA: University of California Press, 1951).

the growth of the faith. In the end, of course, all of the spectacular successes of the first Christians in Japan came to naught with the expulsion orders and persecutions which followed the arrival of Tokugawa rule in the early part of the 17th century, until by the 1630's the Christian religion had all but been eliminated from the country. The efforts begun by Xavier then ultimately failed in Japan, and for reasons which were in part perhaps already apparent during the period of his own, brief tenure there. Nevertheless, his place in Japanese history, as the first missionary at the beginning of a period of extraordinary, if short-lived, Christian influence, cannot be denied. Likewise his successes in other areas, most notably on the southern coast of India, are indisputable. Xavier was formally canonized a saint of the Roman Catholic Church in 1622.

STUDY/DISCUSSION QUESTIONS FOR
SAINT FRANCIS XAVIER

1. What were the historical forces underway in Europe which brought the Portuguese to Japan in the second half of the 16th century? In what ways does the life and career of Saint Fancis Xavier serve to reflect these forces?

2. What were the historical forces at work in Japan in the second half of the 16th century? How do they help to explain Xavier's experiences there and those of the Catholic missionaries who followed him?

3. What role did the Protestant Reformation in Europe play in the events of the early 17th century in Japan? How did this effect the attempts of the Catholic missionaries to Christianize Japan?

4. What mistakes do you think Xavier and the missionaries who followed him made in their efforts to Christianize Japan? What could they have done differently that might have led to a different outcome?

5. Do you think the effort to Christianize Japan was a good or a bad idea overall? Take into account the *short-term* effects of this effort (in the second half of the 16th century), the *medium-range* effects (in the first half of the 17th century), and the *possible long-term* effects (i.e., the role of Christianity in Japan today).

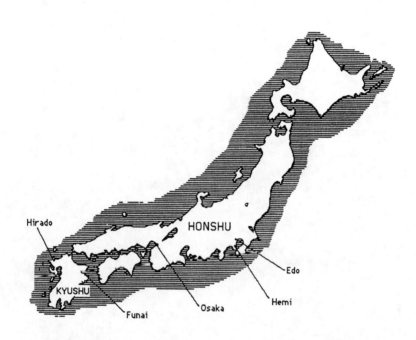

Hirado

HONSHU

KYUSHU

Edo

Funai

Osaka

Hemi

Chapter 2

Will Adams
(1564-1620)

Renaissance Adventurer in Japan

Will (William) Adams, the first Englishman to come to Japan, played an important role as an advisor to the Japanese leader Tokugawa Ieyasu during the final stages of national reunification in the early part of the 17th century. Born in Gillingham, Kent in 1564 into extremely modest circumstances, he seems to have been naturally gifted in a number of areas. He was originally apprenticed as a shipwright, completing his apprenticeship in 1588 in time to play a minor role, as the captain of a supply ship, in the defeat of the Spanish Armada the same year. The following year he married his English wife, Mary Hyn, who soon bore him a daughter. The next decade of his life saw him almost constantly at sea, and 1593 marked the beginning of his association with the Dutch, which would eventually bring him to Japan, when he joined an expedition sponsored by that country to search for a 'northeast passage' to the Orient by sailing through the Arctic Sea. The project failed, but upon returning to Holland in 1595 Adams eventually joined another Dutch expedition, this time to enter the Far Eastern trade in direct competition with Portugal and Spain.

A fleet of five ships left Texel, in Holland, for this purpose in June of 1598 with Adams as the pilot first of the *Hoop* (later lost at sea), and then of the *Die Liefde*. The expedition was ill-fated from the beginning, suffering from delays, poor leadership, and shortage of supplies. After crossing the South Atlantic and passing through the Straits of Magellan the ships were separated by a storm, and only the *Die Liefde* successfully made landfall on the Asian continent. After touching briefly there, the ship prepared to return to South America but the ship's company was attacked by natives on an island where they had landed to take on supplies and this, combined with the fear of Spanish ships in the area, led to the decision to sail to the newly-discovered country of "Iapon." On their way there they encountered another severe storm and on April 19, 1600 they appeared off the eastern coast of Kyushu near the town of Funai (modern day Oita) with only 24 of their original crew of 110 still living, and only six of those able to walk under their own power.

The group arrived in Japan at a crucial juncture. The Japanese leader Tokugawa Ieyasu, following the death of his predecessor Toyotomi Hideyoshi two years earlier, was in the final stages of establishing control over the country. (The Battle of Sekigahara in which he defeated his major remaining rivals occurred in October of that year, and by 1603, three years after Adams' arrival, Ieyasu had assumed the title of *shogun* and the Tokugawa *bakufu* which would rule Japan for the next two and a half centuries had begun.) At the time of the party's arrival Ieyasu was in Osaka and before word could be received from him on the matter, the group, with Adams as their principal spokesperson (because of his familiarity with the Portuguese language), was questioned by several Portuguese brought from Nagasaki. The Portuguese quickly declared the members of the party pirates and heretics because of their Dutch (and Protestant) affiliation. Their probable execution, however, was delayed pending word from Ieyasu. The following month Adams appeared before Ieyasu in Osaka, and the celebrated relationship between the Japanese leader and the English pilot was born.

From the start Ieyasu seems to have been very impressed by Adams, both because of his knowledge of Western technology and culture as well as for the personal qualities he possessed. After confiscating the contents of the Dutch ship, which contained a large amount of military supplies, Ieyasu, curious by nature, sought information from the newcomer concerning Western mathematics, navigation, trade and political affairs. He seems in particular to have appreciated Adams' capacity to discuss these matters without the constant references to religious faith which characterized the discourse of the Portuguese missionaries. Adams for his part offered a view of the missionaries and the Roman Catholic Church which served to cast doubt on the sincerity of their motives. Some of Ieyasu's later reaction against the Portuguese and Spanish missionaries-- in the expulsion edicts and persecutions which occurred in the second decade of the century-- may have been due in part at least to Adams' influence.[1] Within a relatively short period of time Adams had gained Ieyasu's trust and patronage. Among the projects he became involved in soon after his arrival was the construction of a ship using European techniques, and with the subsequent appearance of Dutch and English traders as the new century progressed his offices as a diplomat and trade negotiator were also utilized.

In return for his assistance, Ieyasu provided Adams with a large estate in the village of Hemi (near the modern port of Yokosuka) on the Miura Peninsula south of Ieyasu's center of control at Edo (modern day Tokyo). As a result of successful business ventures, he was also able to purchase a house in the Nihonbashi district of Edo on a street which became known as Anjin-cho, or "The Navigator Street." Adams seems to have had relative freedom of movement within the country and even undertook, beginning in 1608, a series of voyages to other parts of Southeast Asia (to the Philippines, Okinawa, Siam (Thailand) and Cochin-China (Vietnam), but in the early years at least he was refused permission to return to England despite the presence of his wife and daughter there. Over the years he sent money back for their support, made provision for them in his will, and sent a celebrated series of letters back to them which are preserved in the records of the British East India Company, but he never returned to the country of his birth. Eventually taking the name Miura Anjin, a combination of the name of the peninsula where his estate was located and the Japanese word for his pilot's vocation, he became fluent in Japanese, adopted Japanese dress and took a Japanese wife, Magome Kageyu, who bore him two additional children. In later years, when he could have returned to England, he chose not to do so, in part because of differences with the English merchants in Japan who considered him too Japanese-- in their words a "naturalised Japanner"[2]-- and in part one presumes because of the new life he had made for himself in Japan. Despite his differences with the English traders, Adams played a key role in the establishment

[1] Adams seems to have played a role, for example, in convincing Ieyasu that a survey of the Japanese coast by a Spanish ship, for which the Spanish had actually gained prior permission, would in Europe have been considered an act of espionage (Richard Storry, *A History of Modern Japan* (Middlesex, England: Penguin, 1982), p. 62).
[2] From the *Kodansha Encyclopedia of Japan* (Tokyo: Kodansha, 1983), vol. 1, p. 11.

of the English trading station at Hirado in northwestern Kyushu in 1613, and used his influence over the years in behalf of his mother country.

Following the death of Tokugawa Ieyasu in 1616 Adams' influence with the *bakufu* leadership waned. In his last years, as tensions between the English and Dutch mounted over trading rights in Japan and the new *shogun*, Hidetada, began implementing the policies which would lead to the eventual expulsion of all foreigners from the country, Adams did what he could in behalf of English interests. Unfortunately, the Anglo-Dutch treaty which united these two countries in their activities in Japan occurred a few months after his death, and even this event, important as it was, would do little to prevent Japan's eventual move toward seclusion.

Adams became ill and died of an unspecified illness at Hirado on May 16, 1620. The sources are in dispute, however, as to his final resting place. A recent tourist guidebook in Japan states that his ashes are buried near his estate at Hemi, where today a memorial stands commemorating the fact; others, however, suggest that he was actually buried at Hirado and that his grave may have been among those destroyed (with the bones "scattered to the winds") during the later Christian persecutions.[3] Whatever the answer to this question, Adams' place among the romantic figures involved in Japan's first contact with the West has long been a topic of interest. The subject of numerous biographies and fictional accounts, among them James Clavell's 1975 best seller *Shogun* and the later television miniseries created from it, Adams stands as one of the earliest examples of a famous type-- the foreigner who takes Japan as his adopted country (see the later chapter on Lafcadio Hearn in this work as another famous example of this type).

---

[3] See *The New Official Guide to Japan* (Tokyo: Japan National Tourist Organization, 1975), p. 413 and Harold S. Williams, *Shades of the Past, or Indiscreet Tales of Japan* (Tokyo: Tuttle, 1958), p. 326 respectively.

STUDY/DISCUSSION QUESTIONS FOR
WILL ADAMS

1. What were some of the key differences-- in background, temperament, motives, etc.-- between Will Adams and Saint Francis Xavier? In what ways, if any, were they similar? How do their respective backgrounds and the countries with which they were involved help to explain their differences?

2. How would you compare the experiences of Adams and Xavier with the Japanese? Which was more successful in dealing with the Japanese leaders they encountered? In what ways were their methods of dealing with the Japanese different?

3. What factors do you think influenced Adams to remain in Japan even though he had a wife and child back in England?

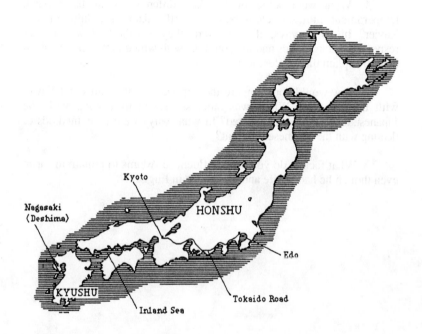

Nagasaki
(Deshima)

Kyoto

HONSHU

KYUSHU

Edo

Inland Sea

Tokaido Road

Chapter 3

Dr. Engelbert Kaempfer
(1651-1716)

Early Observer and Commentator

The German physician, Dr. Engelbert Kaempfer, served at the Dutch trading post of Deshima off the coast of Nagasaki in the late 17th century. His writings about Japan, and especially his monumental *History of Japan* (published posthumously in 1727-28), stand as one of the most important European sources on Japanese life and culture during the Genroku Period (1688-1704).

Kaempfer was born in 1651 in the region which is now North Rhine-Westphalia in Germany. He attended a number of the finest schools and universities of his day in Germany, the Netherlands, Poland and Sweden before entering the service of Sweden as secretary to an embassy to Persia in 1683. When that assignment ended he remained in the region, entering the employment of the Dutch East India Company, and spent the next two years, from 1686 to 1688, in the area surrounding Bandar Abbas (Gombrun) in Persia. By this time also he had begun the process of collecting and compiling information concerning the medical practices, history and culture of the region which, together with his later work on Japan and India, made a major contribution to the existing knowledge of these subjects.

In 1689, still in the employment of the East India Company, he traveled to Batavia (modern day Djakarta, Indonesia) and from there, following a brief stay in Siam (modern day Thailand), he arrived in

Japan in September of 1690. Japan at that time, of course, had entered into the period of national seclusion which was to characterize its history from the early 17th century until the arrival of Commodore Perry and the reopening to the West in the second half of the 19th century. Only the Dutch were allowed to maintain official contact with the country, and their presence was limited to a small trading post, Deshima, located on an island of 130 acres in Nagasaki Harbor on the western side of Kyushu.

Assuming the position of physician at the Dutch post, Kaempfer soon won over the Japanese natives assigned there by providing them with medical treatment and free liquor. One in particular he trained in the Dutch language, and by such means he was able to collect a considerable amount of material on Japanese history and culture despite the official ban on foreigners obtaining such information. In addition, in both 1691 and 1692, Kaempfer accompanied the leader of the Dutch station on his then annual trip to Edo *(Edo sampu)* to offer tribute to the Tokugawa authorities. This undertaking, which involved a journey of several months duration, first by boat through the Inland Sea and then overland along the famous, 300-mile Tokaido Road stretching from Kyoto to Edo, and back again, allowed Kaempfer an excellent opportunity to observe everyday life in Japan at firsthand, an opportunity he took full advantage of in his writings.

Kaempfer's accounts of the trips to Edo, recorded in great detail in his *History,* make fascinating reading. At the outset, of course, there was the problem of selecting the gifts to be taken, many of which had to be purchased at great expense from the local authorities in Nagasaki who purported to know what would be considered appropriate by the Edo officials (but also served as a money-making venture for them). Next came the arrangements for travel. A party of approximately 150 Japanese was needed to accompany the four Dutch officials who customarily made the journey, and since the Dutch preferred to take their own food with them rather than eat the local cuisine a considerable store of European foods as well as eating and cooking utensils also had to be packed. During the overland portion of the trip the Dutch traveled in a highly formal manner, with the head of the post and the top Japanese official who accompanied him riding in cars (or palanquins) carried by bearers, the others on horseback alongside, and the flag and coat of arms of the Dutch East India Company prominently displayed at all times. Every inch of the journey was closely supervised and no deviation from the route of earlier trips, in terms of stopping places, etc., was permitted. The people encountered along the route impressed Kaempfer as polite and well-mannered except for young boys who sometimes yelled insults at them as they passed, and the amount of traffic along the road in his view surpassed at peak times that of the great urban thoroughfares of Europe. In addition to the occasional passage of great *daimyo* and their entourages, which sometimes numbered over a thousand, on their way to and from Edo in connection with their *sankin kotai* (alternate year attendance at the *shogun's* court), the Dutch party also passed Shinagawa, the place on the outskirts of Edo where public executions were held, and saw the heads of the dead left on display as a warning to other would-be lawbreakers ("a very shocking sight" he recorded).[1]

Upon arriving in Edo the group experienced (on one of the trips) a small earthquake and a fire which claimed 600 homes, both of which were fairly frequent occurrences in the city, before being taken for their formal appearance before the *shogun*. This latter involved the ceremony known to the Europeans as 'kowtow,' in which the head of the post moved forward on hands and knees through the gifts to be presented, bowed with his forehead touching the ground to the Japanese leader, and then "crawled backward [again] like a crab without uttering a single word."[2] In the years that Kaempfer made the journey this event was followed by another, before the ladies of the court, during which the members of the company were required to perform-- sing, dance, speak in Japanese and Dutch, and execute other "apish tricks"[3]-- while the women watched from behind bamboo screens or curtains. Kaempfer also was asked to provide free medical consultation. Before leaving Edo the party was taken to the homes of various local officials to put on similar shows, then back to the court for a formal reading of the official orders regarding their continued presence in Japan, including the prohibition against bringing any Portuguese priests or missionaries into the country. After receiving gifts in return from the court-- thirty Japanese kimonos on the occasion of one of the trips-- and attending a banquet which the Dutch, with their European tastes, thought quite terrible, they were allowed to depart on their return journey.

In addition to the descriptions of Japanese history and culture obtained from the Japanese at Deshima and his detailed accounts of the annual *Edo sampu*, Kaempfer was also successful in accumulating, during his two years in Japan (and despite the ban on foreigners obtaining such materials), a large collection of books and other items

---

[1]George Sansom, *A History of Japan, 1615-1867* (Tokyo: Tuttle, 1974), p. 136.
[2]From Harold S. Williams, *Shades of the Past, or Indiscreet Tales of Japan* (Tokyo: Tuttle, 1958), p. 43.
[3]*Ibid.*

representative of the culture of the period. These materials, which provide an excellent sampling of Japanese life and culture during the Genroku Period, are now housed in the British Museum in London. Of the Japanese themselves, Kaempfer seems to have had the highest regard, writing in 1692 that they are: "Bold ... heroic ... revengeful ... desirous of fame ... very industrious and enured to hardship ... great lovers of civility and good manners, and very nice in keeping themselves, their cloaths and houses, clean and neat...."[4] Or on another occasion, that they are "[u]nited and peaceable, taught to give due worship to the gods, due obedience to the Laws, due submission to their superiors, due love and regard to their neighbours."[5] In a controversial essay included in his *History* he also argued in support of Japan's seclusion policy, concluding that the land "was never in a happier condition than it now is, governed by an arbitrary monarch, shut up, and kept from all commerce and communication with foreign nations."[6]

Kaempfer left Japan in November of 1692 and returned to Europe where he did further medical studies at Leiden before returning to his home region in Germany to become the physician to a local prince. Over the years he continued to write and publish on a variety of medical and cultural topics. He died in 1716 at the age of 65, leaving behind a truly impressive array of work, including his great work on Japan. Following Kaempfer's departure from Japan several other famous physicians-- among them Dr. Carl Thunberg, a Swedish doctor there from 1775 to 1776, and Dr. Philipp Franz von Siebold, a German who lived in Japan from 1823 to 1830-- carried on his tradition of cultural study and observation, but Kaempfer's role as the first of a unique and interesting breed places him in a position of clear preeminence among this type of early Westerner in Japan.

---

[4] Quoted in Harold S. Williams, *Foreigners in Mikadoland* (Tokyo: Tuttle, 1963), p. 7.
[5] Quoted in G.B. Sansom, *The Western World and Japan; A Study in the Interaction of European and Asiatic Cultures* (Tokyo: Tuttle, 1977), p. 188.
[6] From the *Kodansha Encyclopedia of Japan* (Tokyo: Kodansha, 1983), vol. 4, p. 102. Rather interestingly, after copies of Kaempfer's *History* made their way back to Japan in the 18th century, this essay was translated and used by individuals such as Shizuki Tadao (1760-1806), a well-known student of Western learning (*rangaku*), to support their arguments for continuation of the seclusion policy (*Ibid.*).

STUDY/DISCUSSION QUESTIONS FOR
DR. ENGELBERT KAEMPFER

1. Why does Kaempfer's work constitute such a unique and important source for our knowledge of Japan during late 17th century?

2. How would you contrast Kaempfer's personality with those of Saint Francis Xavier or Will Adams? What were his chief reasons for going to Japan?

3. What was the attitude regarding foreigners in Japan during the time of Kaempfer's stay there?

4. What important intellectual trends were underway in Europe during the period of Kaempfer's stay in Japan which Japan, as a result of its official policy of isolation, missed? In what ways did Kaempfer himself symbolize these trends? What was the long-term effect of this intellectual isolation on Japan?

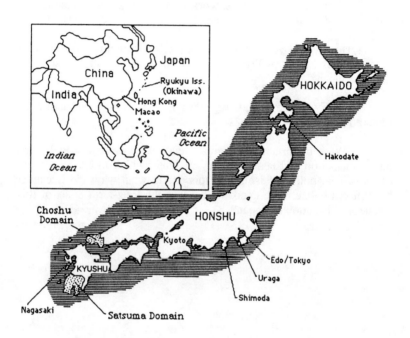

Chapter 4

Commodore Matthew C. Perry (1794-1858)

Re-Opening Japan to the West

Commodore Matthew C. Perry was the American naval officer whose arrival in Japan in 1853 played a key role in the reopening of Japan to the West after over two centuries of isolation, and helped to set in motion the series of events leading to the Meiji Restoration and the modernization of the country in the second half of the 19th century. Born in Kingston, Rhode Island in 1794, Perry was the younger brother of Oliver Hazard Perry (1785-1819), American naval hero of the War of 1812. Prior to coming to Japan the younger Perry had served with distinction in a number of distant places, including assignments with the Mediterranean, African and West Indian naval squadrons. From 1837 to 1840 he commanded the first U.S. steamship, the *Fulton*, and during the Mexican War (1846-48) he was the chief planner of the seige of Veracruz (1847), often considered his most brilliant strategic achievement, although overshadowed in historical importance by his later voyage to Japan. By the early 1850's he had acquired an almost legendary reputation, known among his men as "Old Matt" and "Old Bruin" for the strictness of his discipline, and by the political leaders of the day as a strong supporter of naval innovation and reform (among his causes were the use of steam for naval ships, the use of the shell gun to replace the older type of naval gunnery, and the establishment of a U.S. naval academy). When then President Millard Fillmore determined in 1851 that the expedition to Japan, long requested and lobbied for by shipping and commercial interests in the U.S., should be undertaken, Perry was a logical choice for the command.

Japan, since the early part of the 17th century, had been almost completely cut off from the West. Only the Dutch, located on the small island of Deshima in Nagasaki harbor, had been allowed to maintain a highly-regulated contact and trade. Although periodic attempts to reopen the country had been made, most notably by the Russians as early as the second quarter of the 18th century and with increasing frequency in the first half of the 19th century, none of these efforts had succeeded. (A British expedition in 1813-14 had also failed, as had an earlier American attempt led by Commodore James Biddle in 1846-- Commodore Biddle, in addition, had allowed himself (and by extension his country) to be insulted when he was pushed by a Japanese sailor and failed to seek appropriate redress. A Russian expedition under Vice Admiral E. V. Putiatin arrived in Japan a month after Perry, adding its weight to the growing pressure on the Japanese authorities.)

In addition to the matter of trade, the Japanese were also notorious for their mistreatment of foreign sailors shipwrecked or otherwise cast onto their shores, including among other outrages, placing them (in the words of one author) in "prison cages, which contraptions were not unlike the circus cages in which wild animals are... confined, except that they were made of bamboo and were not nearly so commodious and far less comfortable." Even Japanese sailors shipwrecked in other countries were not allowed to return to their homeland for fear of it providing an excuse for other nations to violate Japan's self-imposed isolation-- as one document of a slightly earlier period stated, "...it being the law of Japan that such persons cease to be Japanese and become the subjects of that government into whose hand destiny had cast them..."[1] In line with these concerns then, the specific purposes of Perry's expedition were threefold: first, to obtain from Japan a pledge concerning the humane treatment of shipwrecked sailors; second (and following from the first), to gain the opening of at least one Japanese port for the provision and fueling of foreign ships; and third, in line with the larger issue of growing Western commercial interests in the region, to seek the opening of one or more ports to foreign trade.

Aware of the earlier failures, and with the pride of his young and rapidly-expanding nation at stake, Perry was prepared to use force if necessary to achieve his ends. He arrived with a total of four ships (two

---

[1]Harold S. Williams, *Foreigners in Mikadoland* (Tokyo: Tuttle, 1963), pp. 34-5; 82.

steam-powered warships and two smaller sailing vessels)-- referred to collectively as the "black ships" by the Japanese-- at Uraga at the mouth of Edo (Tokyo) Bay on July 8, 1853. With a considerable display of pomp and ceremony (and a retinue of 300 armed marines) Perry presented the presidential letter, his own credentials and a personal letter to the local authorities in which he stated that although his intentions were peaceful he fully expected to carry out his mission and would take whatever steps were necessary to accomplish it. Having completed this initial stage of the assignment, he informed the authorities that he would return the following spring with an even larger force to receive their answer, and then departed for Hong Kong and Macao on the China coast where he spent the fall and early winter months.

Although Perry's arrival was by no means a total surprise to the Japanese (advance word had been received from Okinawa in the Ryukyu Islands south of Japan where Perry had landed prior to proceeding to Edo), it occurred at a critical juncture in Japanese history. The exisiting government, the Tokugawa *bakufu* established by Tokugawa Ieyasu in the early part of the 17th century and in power for the previous 250 years, had been in a weakened state for some time, beset by internal as well as external difficulties. In addition to the threat represented by the Western nations, powerful *daimyo* (regional political leaders) who lived at some distance from the central government in Edo-- most notably in Satsuma in southern Kyushu and Choshu at the western end of Honshu-- had risen to challenge the central authority. Perry's arrival then precipitated a crisis of internal as well as external significance for the *bakufu* leaders, requiring a forceful response both in terms of dealing with the external events themselves and as a sign to these regional leaders that it was still in control and able to take effective action. The Tokugawa leadership, as it turned out, was not up to the task. Caught between a growing sentiment in the outer regions favoring resistance to the West, but with its own awareness (reinforced by the arrival of Perry) of the military superiority of the Western powers, the central government decided to take the unprecedented step of seeking advice on the matter from the *daimyo*. The chief advisor to the *shogun*, Abe Masahiro (1819-1857), at that time the most powerful individual in the government due to the decline in the office of *shogun* itself, had a translated copy of the letter from the U.S. president sent to all major *daimyo* as well as prominent Confucian scholars and other government officials. This in itself, however, was seen by the regional leaders as a sign of weakness, and when the central government subsequently gravitated toward a position of at least temporary capitulation to the Western demands a further stage in its decline had been reached.

Perry, unaware of the internal crisis his initial appearance had set off, returned to the country the following February with the larger fleet he had promised-- a total of nine ships this time, including three steam-powered frigates with black smoke pouring from their stacks. With no other choice available to them, the Tokugawa leadership soon agreed to the terms of the Treaty of Kanagawa, signed on March 31, 1854. The treaty pledged Japan to humane treatment of shipwrecked sailors, and granted the U.S. "most-favored-nation" status-- an idea which had emerged from Great Britain's treaties with China some years earlier, automatically giving, to the U.S. in this case, terms similar to those of any other country which might subsequently negotiate a more favorable treaty with Japan. In addition, the treaty opened two ports (Shimoda on the Izu Peninsula southwest of modern day Tokyo and Hakodate on the northern island of Hokkaido) to American ships, and while it did not formally open trade between the two countries it provided for the possibility of the opening of a consulate at Shimoda within 18 months. (Some disagreement seems to have existed on this latter point, with the Japanese text of the treaty indicating that this would occur only if both nations desired it, while the U.S. version left it up to the wishes of either country alone.)

Once the terms of the treaty had been agreed upon the two sides formally exchanged gifts, symbolizing in effect the priorities and values of their respective cultures: the Japanese providing items considered of high aesthetic value (silks, porcelains, items done in gold lacquer), the Americans, items of a more pragmatic sort. Among the latter were a collection of military weapons (rifles, pistols, swords), books such as *Webster's Dictionary* and Audubon's *The Birds of America*, small, working models of a train and telegraph, and a considerable amount of alcoholic spirits of various types. While the Americans seem to have been somewhat disappointed at what they considered the paucity of the Japanese items, the American gifts were a source of great interest to the Japanese, some of whom displayed at least some prior knowledge of Western technology and science, gained, no doubt, through the tradition of *rangaku*-- Dutch, or Western, studies-- carried on in Japan through contact with the Dutch in Deshima.[2] The working models of the telegraph and railroad, the latter large enough to ride on, were of particular interest, but even more so were the handguns included among

---

[2] At first this had been done surreptitiously but when the ban on such study was lifted in 1720 it had been carried forward with considerable vigor.

the collection of Western firearms.[3] The Japanese also showed considerable interest in the clothing and other equipment of the Americans, staring, touching, and making copious notes and drawings of it. Some *samurai* even came secretly to the American ships at night, risking certain death at the hands of the local authorities, and asked to be taken to the West to learn more of its ways and culture. Finally, a variety of popular entertainments-- an exhibition of *sumo* by the Japanese and a minstrel show put on by the Americans-- accompanied by ample amounts of alcohol provided by both sides, brought this initial encounter between the two countries to a close. Although Perry's arrival was to have enormous long-term significance for Japan, setting off a chain of events which would effect virtually every aspect of Japanese life, the immediate scene seems to have ended on a positive note.

Perry left Japan soon after and never returned. His arrival back in the U.S. in 1855 saw him feted in Washington, brought him a considerable amount of national acclaim and gained him recognition as an expert on Far Eastern affairs, although his larger recommendations on the subject (urging the U.S. to acquire island bases in the region to offset British and Russian expansion there) were not followed through on until later in the century. He died in 1858, just as he was being considered for command of the prestigious Mediterranean squadron, a much sought-after position.

Following Perry's departure from Japan, other Western countries-- Great Britain in October of 1854, Russia in February of 1855 and Holland in November of the same year-- negotiated treaties with terms roughly similar to the American treaty, thus setting the scene for the later Ansei Treaties (also known as the "Unequal" Treaties[4]) between Japan and a number of other Western countries which plagued Japan for the next half century. Following his departure as well, the processes of

---

[3]Guns, of course, were not unknown in Japan at that time, having been introduced initially by the Portuguese in the 16th century and playing a role of some significance in the late 16th century battles which brought about the reunification of the country. Strangely (and rather uniquely, considering the history of firearms in other places once they have been introduced) their use had gradually faded out in Japan during the Edo Period, the Japanese *samurai* preferring the use of the sword, and the long period of peace following the establishment of the Tokugawa *bakufu* rendering them less of a necessity. (See Noel Perrin, *Giving Up the Gun, Japan's Reversion to the Sword, 1543-1879* (Boulder, Colo.: Shambhala, 1980) for an interesting account of this subject.)

[4]Unequal because Japan, like most other non-Western countries of the day, was not recognized as an equal partner in them.

internal change which his appearance had set into motion continued their inexorable sweep toward the overthrow of the Tokugawa government and the creation of a new political order following the Meiji Restoration in 1867. Although it would be wrong to say that Perry's arrival in Japan 'caused' these events, it nevertheless clearly served as a catalyst for them. Nothing in Japan would ever be quite the same again. In 1856 Townsend Harris arrived in the country as its first American ambassador. To this latter individual came the task of following up on the process of establishing permanent relations which Perry had begun, a far more difficult assignment than Perry's as subsequent events reveal.

STUDY/DISCUSSION QUESTIONS FOR
COMMODORE MATTHEW C. PERRY

1. What were the historical forces at work in the West in the middle of the 19th century which led to Commodore Perry's trip to Japan?

2. How would you describe the rules of international behavior in the middle of the 19th century as they pertain to Perry's trip? What gave Perry the right to *force* Japan to open up to the West? In what ways have the rules of international behavior changed since that time?

3. In what ways does Perry represent yet another distinct personality type from that of Xavier, Adams or Kaempfer?

4. What effects did Perry's visit have on the internal political situation in Japan in the mid-19th century? How would you describe Perry's role in the events, such as the Meiji Restoration, which followed? Was he a *cause*, an *effect*, or a *catalyst* for these changes? Would Japan's subsequent development have been different if Perry had not come?

5. What did Perry represent to the Japanese? How did the style he effected, even the gifts he brought, as well as his general manner of dealing with the Japanese leadership contribute to this image?

Chapter 5

Townsend Harris
(1804-1878)

Romance and Reality in Early U.S.-Japan Diplomatic Relations

To Townsend Harris was given the task of following up on the establishment of permanent relations between the United States and Japan begun by Commodore Perry's famous trip. A prominent New York merchant, educational reformer and member of the local Democratic Party, Harris left his home city in 1849 following a quarrel with his brother over business matters and traveled to the Far East to investigate commercial prospects in the region. During the next six years he traveled extensively in China and other parts of Southeast Asia, and, after being rebuffed in his efforts to secure a diplomatic post in China in 1854, used his political influence in the Democratic administration of President Franklin Pierce to gain the appointment as the first consul general to Japan. He arrived in Japan to assume this post in August of 1856.

Whereas Perry had come with a full display of military might, Harris' arrival in Shimoda (where the consulate, according to the Treaty of Kanagawa, was to be situated) was a much less auspicious affair. Shimoda was a small fishing village, located some distance from the seat of the government at Edo. There Harris and his small party, which included a young Dutch interpreter named Henry Heusken[1] and two

---

[1]Dutch, rather than English, was the chief European language of which the Japanese had knowledge at that time. Heusken himself makes an interesting subject for study. A man with a considerable fondness for women, and

Chinese servants, were housed in a local Buddhist temple, and Harris
sought to accomplish his first order of business, the delivery of a letter
from the President of the United States to the Japanese Emperor. Harris'
Journal records his difficulties in carrying out this assignment. The
Japanese authorities seem to have had little interest in facilitating the
process of exchange. A portion of his entry for September 9th, 1856,
reads: "I am determined to take firm ground with the Japanese. I will
cordially meet any offers of amity, but words will not do. They are the
greatest liars on earth," and two days later, on the 11th: "Had a flare-up
with the officials who told me some egregious lies." During the period
of 14 months that he waited to carry out his assignment, Harris
occupied himself by reading whatever materials he could find on Japan,
including the works written by Dr. Kaempfer more than a century and a
half before. He also made his own attempts at studying the local flora
and fauna, but once again was thwarted by the local officials. (In a
Journal entry from May of 1857 he writes: "I am collecting specimens
of natural history, but they are meagre, as the Japanese will not bring
me [even] one, on the national principle of concealing everything.")
During this period also he suffered from persistent ill health which
would plague him throughout his tenure in Japan, losing 40 pounds
during his first six months in the country, and finally reaching the
point of appointing his interpreter, Heusken, vice-counsel in order that
the mission might be carried forward in the event of his death. As if
these problems were not enough, he received little support or guidance
from the U.S. officials at home, at one point even running short of
money and being "reduced [in his own words] to the mortifying
necessity of asking credit from the Japanese for necessary daily
supplies." (On another occasion [April 25, 1857] he writes: "My last
letters from the Department of State were dated in October, 1855, more
than eighteen months ago. It is too long a period to leave me here
alone, and some order should be given to ensure more frequent
communication with me.") His overall state of mind during these first
months in Japan are perhaps best summed up in a *Journal* entry written
at the time of his first Christmas in the country in 1856: "Merry
Christmas! How happy are those who live in lands where those joyous
greetings can be exchanged! As for me, I am sick and solitary, living,
as one may say, in a prison; a large one it is true but still a prison."[2]

involved in a number of incidents connected with the history of this period,
he was murdered by a *ronin* (or masterless *samurai*) in 1861.
[2]These quotations from Harris' *Journal* are from Harold S. Williams, *Shades
of the Past, or Indiscreet Tales of Japan* (Tokyo: Tuttle, 1958), pp. 82, 38;
[same author], *Foreigners in Mikadoland* (Tokyo: Tuttle, 1963), pp. 49, 48-

Despite the formidable obstacles before him, Harris eventually obtained his meeting with the Japanese *shogun* at the latter's headquarters at Edo in December of 1857. (He seems to have believed that this individual was actually the emperor, not understanding the complexities of the Japanese system whereby the *shogun*, or military head of the country, ruled in behalf of an emperor who resided in obscurity at the old capital of Kyoto). Even once the meeting had been agreed to, following months of foot-dragging and procrastination, the precise details under which it would be conducted-- the manner in which Harris would travel, the degree of deference that he would display to the Japanese leader, etc.-- required an additional period of negotiation. In addition, preparations for the meeting on the American side, in order to provide the proper degree of dignity for the occasion (the decoration of clothing, uniforms and other accoutrements with the Seal of the U.S., the assembling of gifts to be presented) required much work with extremely limited resources. Finally, however, the party left Shimoda for the 7-day journey to Edo, Harris and Heusken riding on horseback behind the American flag and accompanied by approximately 150 Japanese officials and their servants and retainers. The famous Tokkaido Road, earlier described in the works of Dr. Kaempfer as a bustling and colorful thoroughfare, had been completely cleared of traffic and freshly swept for the occasion with all of its side roads and entrances sealed off with straw ropes. Throughout the journey, and into the audience chamber itself (where he followed his custom of putting on new patent-leather shoes rather than proceeding onto the *tatami* in his stocking feet), Harris maintained a constant effort to uphold *his* perception at least of the dignity of his country. His own attire, which he had worn on other state occasions in Asia, included "...a coat embroidered with gold[,] blue pantaloons with a broad gold band running down each leg, cocked hat with gold tassels and a pearl handled dress sword." (One author, commenting on this outfit, suggests that its flamboyance may have been one of the factors leading to a Congressional resolution passed a decade later placing stricter limits on the degree of latitude exercised by U.S. diplomats in their choice of ceremonial attire.)[3] In this manner then, although delivering the letter to the *shogun* rather

---

9; and *Shades of the Past...*, p. 103, respectively. In addition to what he perceived as the basic dishonesty of the Japanese officials, Harris also suspected them of secretly opening and reading his mail (*Shades of the Past...*, p. 214).
[3]The description from Harris' *Journal*, as well as the commentary, are from *Foreigners in Mikadoland*, pp. 53-4.

than to the emperor (and from a president who had left office earlier that
same year), Harris carried out the first part of his mission.

Of even greater, long-term importance than the letter was the
negotiation of a commercial treaty following up on Perry's preliminary
treaty (the Treaty of Kanagawa) negotiated three years earlier. To this
task Harris now turned his energies. The "Harris Treaty" as it is
sometimes called was signed on July 29th of the following year (1858).
Among its 14 articles were: the right of the two countries to exchange
diplomats at their respective capitals (a provision lacking in the 1854
treaty and which accounted for at least some of the difficulty Harris had
experienced in obtaining his original meeting with the Japanese
leadership); the opening of several additional ports, among them
Nagasaki, Kanagawa (later replaced by Yokohama), Niigata, and Hyogo
(the modern city of Kobe), to trade and the presence of American
citizens[4]; and the right of Japan to purchase ships and arms from the
U.S., and to hire American military and technical advisors. The treaty
also specifically prohibited the opium trade (a positive element
considering the earlier British policy of forcing this trade on China), but
contained several negative (or "unequal") elements, among them
continued "most-favored-nation" status for the U.S., the concept of
extra-territoriality (whereby American citizens residing in Japan would
be governed by American rather than Japanese law), and a fixed scale of
tariffs between the two nations. The completion of the treaty also set a
precedent for other Western nations eager to open trade with Japan, and
within a matter of weeks England, France, Russia and the Netherlands
had all negotiated treaties with similar elements, thus creating the Ansei
(or "Unequal") treaties noted in the previous chapter.[5]

Harris resided in Japan for another five years following the
completion of the commercial treaty, continuing to be plagued by the
poor health and the periodic problems with the local authorities which
had characterized the earlier part of his stay. During this time he
witnessed firsthand the dramatic changes occurring in the country as a
result of the treaties with the U.S. and the other Western nations.
Foreign settlements in places like Yokohama (formerly a tiny fishing
village) and Hyogo (later to become the great port city of Kobe) grew
rapidly, taking on a colorful atmosphere reminiscent of the mining

---

[4]Edo and Osaka were to be added in 1862 and 1863 respectively.
[5]New treaties with these countries, recognizing Japan as a fully equal partner
and giving it the right in particular to set its own tariff rates, did not come
into existence until 1911. The name Ansei in connection with the original
treaties from the 1850's refers to the name of the emperor's reign during
which they were negotiated and signed.

camps of the American West of approximately the same period.[6] At the same time, the political changes which would bring about the collapse of the Tokugawa *bakufu* and the creation of a new government following the Meiji Restoration in 1867 moved steadily forward. By the time Harris left Japan in May of 1862, Ii Naosuke, the chief Japanese signer of the Ansei treaties, had been assassinated by anti-government forces (in March, 1860), and the process of Tokugawa decline was rapidly accelerating.

One final aspect of the Townsend Harris story requires discussion here, namely the question of his supposed love affair with a Japanese woman named Okichi. Originally given its first romanticized telling by a Japanese doctor named Muramatsu Shunsui close to forty years after the events in question, and further embellished by a popular American novel and film, *The Barbarian and the Geisha*, produced in the years following World War II,[7] this story draws on romantic elements from *both* cultures. In the Japanese version one is given the tragic tale of a young woman who sacrifices herself for the good of her country by being sent to live with Harris when he specifically requests her after seeing her on the street one day following her afternoon bath. The cinematic version, of course, draws upon all the romantic elements of that period in Hollywood filmmaking to create an even more preposterous version of the story.[8] Whatever the final interpretation one chooses regarding the actual truth of this incident, its presence clearly adds an element of sheer romanticism to the far more prosaic reality of Harris' tenure in Japan.

---

[6]See the works of Harold S. Williams cited above for popular accounts of this topic.

[7]Both the novel, authored by Robert Payne, and the film, which starred John Wayne as Harris, were produced in 1958.

[8]The Japanese version is discussed in Oliver Statler's *Shimoda Story* (Tokyo: Tuttle, 1971), pp. 384ff.; the American cinematic version in Harold S. Williams' essay entitled "The Townsend Harris Calumny" in *Foreigners in Makadoland*, pp. 40-56. Williams tends to discount the possibility of any manner of sexual relationship between Harris and Okichi, while Statler accepts it, albeit in a far more realistic manner than either country's romanticized retelling of the incident.

STUDY/DISCUSSION QUESTIONS FOR
TOWNSEND HARRIS

1. In what ways was Townsend Harris' task considerably more difficult than that of Perry? How can one best explain the behavior of the Japanese toward Harris during the initial stages of his residence in Japan? In what manner did Harris seek to uphold the dignity of his home country during his meeting with the Japanese *shogun* in December of 1857?

2. What were the terms of the treaty which Harris finally negotiated with the Japanese in July of 1858? In what ways was this treaty good for Japan? What were its chief liabilities from the Japanese perspective?

3. What were some of the changes which occurred in Japan during the years from 1856 to 1862 that Harris resided there?

4. The story of Harris' supposed love affair with a Japanese woman has been given expression in the popular culture of both countries. How does each country's 'version' of the story serve to reflect the attitudes and values of the respective cultures?

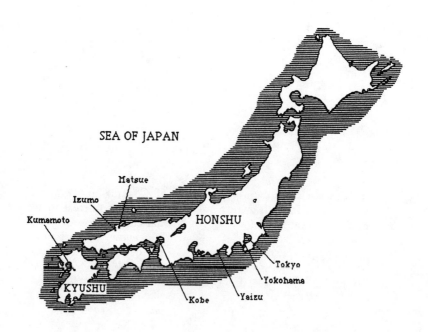

SEA OF JAPAN

Matsue

Izumo

Kumamoto

HONSHU

KYUSHU

Tokyo

Yokohama

Kobe

Yaizu

Chapter 6

Lafcadio Hearn
(1850-1904)

Homeless Wanderer and Interpreter of Japanese Culture

In the decades following the arrival of Commodore Perry and Townsend Harris, Japan became a subject of enormous interest to the peoples of the West. In the arts and in popular culture especially, the interest in Japan, refracted through the late 19th century fascination for the exotic and the picturesque, became a kind of international craze. Painters from the French Impressionist Manet to the Expressionist Bonnard utilized Japanese themes in their work, and popular composers of the day created highly-romanticized depictions of Japanese life ranging from Gilbert and Sullivan's *Mikado* (1885) to Giacomo Puccini's *Madame Butterfly* (1904). Numerous writers also tackled the subject of Japan, creating works ranging in style from Pierre Loti's romantic novel, *Madame Chrysanthemum* in 1888, to the more scholarly studies of Basil Hall Chamberlain (*Things Japanese* - 1890). Among these early literary interpreters of Japan, none perhaps has enjoyed such a wide and continuing interest as Lafcadio Hearn, the strange, disquieted, end-of-the-century figure, who one recent biographer has described as a 'wandering ghost'.[1]

---

[1]Jonathan Cott, *Wandering Ghost: The Odyssey of Lafcadio Hearn* (New York: Alfred A. Knopf, 1990).

The dual themes of abandonment and loss characterized Hearn's early years and profoundly affected his later life and work. He was born in 1850 on the Greek island of Lefkas, the child of a Greek mother and an Anglo-Irish father. His father, a British army surgeon, moved the family to Ireland in 1852, but the marriage soon failed and Hearn's mother returned to her homeland, leaving Hearn to be raised by her husband's family. He never saw his mother again. He spent the next several years in the care of an elderly great-aunt, a wealthy but childless widow who had little experience with children, and in 1862 was sent off to the first of two boarding schools, both strict Catholic institutions, where the essential loneliness of his early years continued.[2] It was at the second of these that he suffered an injury to his left eye which eventually cost him his sight in the eye. The blind left eye, together with a right eye which protruded slightly from birth and grew more protrusive over time as it compensated for the blind eye, gave him a kind of bug-eyed appearance and was a lifelong source of embarrassment to him. His weak eyes also forced him to do close work with the use of a magnifying glass or by holding the material up within a few inches of his face, and to have at best only indistinct distant vision. His formal education ended in 1867 when a distant relative who had assumed control of the great-aunt's affairs went bankrupt, and in 1869 this individual decided to free himself of any further responsibility for the young man by sending him off to America to live. In the spring of that year he bought Lafcadio, then eighteen, a one-way ticket to Cincinnati where he had a relative who he said would help him to get established. Thus began the series of travels or 'wanderings' which would eventually bring Lafcadio Hearn to Japan.

The relative in Cincinnati proved to be of little assistance, and after a brief period of living on the streets and working at a series of temporary jobs, Hearn embarked on a journalistic career as a reporter for the Cincinnati *Enquirer*. He followed this vocation there for the next eight years, demonstrating a penchant for the bizarre and the grotesque, producing articles on the seemy, lower-class life of the city with its sometimes sensational crimes and scandals, and in his spare time

---

[2]His experience in Catholic schools helped to instill in Hearn a lifelong antipathy to the Christian religion, to the extent that he could write in one of his works on Japan *(Japan: An Attempt at Interpretation* - 1904) that "...the Jesuit effort [in the late 16th and early 17th centuries] to Christianize Japan must be regarded as a crime against humanity, a labour of devastation, a calamity comparable only,--by the destruction it wrought,-- to an earthquake, a tidal-wave, a volcanic eruption" (Tuttle edition, 1955, p. 328).

reading and translating the works of several of the newer French authors of the day (Gautier, Anatole France, Flaubert, Maupassant). In 1877, following a brief and controversial marriage to a mulatto woman (at a time when interracial marriages were illegal in that area), he moved to New Orleans, in search also of a more exotic cultural milieu in which to pursue his literary interests. He continued his journalistic career there, and began writing books as well, among them translations and adaptations of foreign literature and a number of works on New Orleans history and culture. In 1889 he published the first of two highly-successful novels, *Chita,* a work with a Louisiana setting. By the time of the publication of this latter work, however, he had once again felt the need to renew his quest for the new and the exotic. This time his travels took him to the French West Indies where he spent the years from 1887 to 1889, once again producing articles and books on the region, among the latter, his second novel, *Youma,* the story of a slave rebellion published in 1890. Upon his return to the U.S. in 1889 he conceived the idea for what was to be his last and most significant journey-- to Japan.

Hearn's interest in Japan dated from at least the mid-1880's when he had covered the Japanese exhibit at the New Orleans Exposition (1884-85) for *Harper's Weekly* and *Harper's Bazaar.* His *Some Chinese Ghosts* (1887), which consisted, as the title suggests, of the retelling of several Chinese ghost stories, also demonstrated an early interest in the literature and culture of the Orient. In 1890, with only an unwritten promise from his New York publisher regarding the book he proposed to write about his experiences, he embarked for Japan.

One of his biographers has written that a search for his own lost childhood characterized Hearn's initial response to all of the places he visited.[3] His arrival in Japan was no exception. In a famous sketch entitled "My First Day in the Orient" (later included as the opening chapter of *Glimpses of Unfamiliar Japan* in 1894) Hearn records his first reactions as he was pulled in a *kuruma* (Japanese rickshaw) around the city of Yokohama, his port of arrival. The sketch includes a myriad of rapid, sensory impressions, all seen through a "beauty of ghostly haze" which the same biographer suggests was the result of Hearn's "myopic eyes... coincidently mirror[ing] the Japanese esthetic of ambiguous beauty."[4] Phrases such as "fantastic prettiness," "amazing picturesqueness," "fairy-land" and "World of Elves" appear throughout

[3]Cott, p. 241.
[4]*Ibid.*

the piece, attesting to this idyllic, first reaction.[5] Making the specific connection to his own past, Hearn wrote to a friend in Cincinnati: "Here I am in the land of dreams-- surrounded by strange Gods. I seem to have known and loved them somewhere before."[6]

In the weeks following his arrival in Japan he settled into the far more mundane activity of finding a way to maintain himself in his new home, for within a short period of time he had quarreled with his editor at Harper's and was without apparent means of support. He now drew upon a letter of introduction he had been given to Basil Hall Chamberlain, another early Western interpreter of Japan and then a professor at Tokyo University, and through Chamberlain's efforts managed to secure a teaching position at a middle school in Matsue, located on the opposite side of the country on the Japan Sea. There in the summer of 1890 he moved to begin his career as a teacher. Although he remained at Matsue for only a year and a half the experience there was to prove an extremely important one for him. Matsue was located close to one of the country's oldest centers of culture, Izumo, and was sufficiently removed from the processes of modernization underway in the larger cities on the eastern side of Japan to allow him to experience firsthand the country's older, more traditional culture. Soon even his writing style, previously characterized by the ornate, rather overdone quality of late 19th century Western prose, had begun to move toward a greater simplicity and restraint in the Japanese manner. It was at Matsue also that he took a Japanese wife. During his first winter in Japan-- an often brutal experience for foreigners given the light construction of Japanese houses and their lack, by Western standards at least, of proper means of heat-- Hearn came down with a serious respiratory ailment. Visiting him during this period, the Japanese principal at his school proposed a long-term solution to his difficulties, marriage to a Japanese woman to look after him. The man subsequently introduced Hearn to Koizumi Setsuko, the

---

[5]Cott includes the entire text of "My First Day in the Orient" in his work (pp. 242-58), from which these phrases are taken.

[6]*Ibid.*, p. 259. Somewhat ironically too, given the subsequent course of his experiences in Japan, Hearn's initial reaction also contains the seeds of future disillusionments. In presenting a series of juxtapositions of the new and the old (e.g., "a shop of American sewing-machines next to the shop of a maker of Buddhist images"), he writes in "My First Day..." of the inevitable "regret" of "[the] traveler who enters suddenly into a period of social change [for] the decay of things beautiful and the ugliness of things new" (in Cott, p. 245).

daughter of a local *samurai*, whom he took as his wife in January of 1891. Although Hearn had been married once before, during the early years in Cincinnati, and had had a number of liaisons with other women during the course of his travels, it was with this Japanese woman that he formed his most lasting relationship. For the next fourteen years, until his death in 1904, he assumed the full reponsibilities of husband and parent, fathering four children by her, assuming the support of her extended family, and even taking her family name (so that today he is known to most Japanese by his adopted name, Koizumi Yakumo, rather than as Lafcadio Hearn). Although Hearn never fully learned Japanese nor she English the two communicated in a kind of combined English and Japanese understandable only to them, and in addition to performing the role of a traditional Japanese wife (handing him his clothes item by item as he dressed in the morning, walking a proper distance behind him when they appeared in public) she also assisted him in some of his later literary projects, most notably his efforts at collecting Japanese ghost stories and folklore.

Along with his teaching duties at Matsue, and later at Kumamoto (a somewhat larger city on the western side of the southern Japanese island of Kyushu) where he took another, better paying position in 1891, Hearn continued his attempts to capture Japan in his writing. His first book-length work on the subject, *Glimpses of Unfamiliar Japan*, a collection of twenty-seven essays opening with the already-mentioned "My First Day in the Orient", was published in 1894, and from that point on he produced a steady stream of books, magazine articles, letters, and other writings on the subject. Always retaining his interest in the exotic and the bizarre-- Japanese folktales and ghost stories became a special interest in his later years-- his investigations into other aspects of traditional Japanese culture, especially Japanese aesthetics and religion, continue to be highly-regarded.[7]

Following three years in Kumamoto, Hearn moved with his family to the city of Kobe in 1894, where he worked briefly as an editorial writer and journalist for the *Kobe Chronicle*, an English language newspaper headquartered there, and then in 1895 he assumed his last teaching position, as a Professor of English Language and Literature at Tokyo University. He held this latter position until 1903 when he was forced out in a move by a new president of that institution

---

[7]See, for example, the quotations from several contemporary writers, both Western and Japanese, quoted in Cott, p. xvii.

to reduce the number of foreigners on its faculty.[8] During these years, despite his strong support and attachment to his adopted country-- he produced essays upholding Japan's militarism in the years preceding the Russo-Japanese War (1904-05) and had even taken Japanese citizenship in 1895-- his intitial euphoria regarding it gradually cooled, particularly in the years following the move from Kumamoto. The realization of the impossibility of ever truly 'becoming' Japanese, despite his Japanese citizenship, seems to have set in, and this, combined with the increasing evidence of modernization and the disappearance of traditional culture in both Kobe and Tokyo where he spent his last years, contributed to his feelings of disillusionment. Despite his growing disenchantment, however, he continued his efforts to capture Japan in his writing, and after losing his post at Tokyo University devoted much of his time to a series of lectures he had been invited to give at Cornell University in New York on the subject of Japan. This work, completed but never presented in lecture form, was to stand as his last and most systematic treatment of the subject, the somewhat dated but still interesting and insightful, *Japan: An Attempt at Interpretation*, published posthumously in 1904.

Although still only in his early fifties, Hearn's health declined markedly after 1902, and he died of heart failure in Tokyo on September 26, 1904. He was buried in a small Buddhist cemetery there, with his Japanese name-- Koizumi Yakumo-- inscribed on the tombstone.

Hearn's writings on Japan, as well as his fourteen-year residence there during the critical period of modernization and reopening to the West, continue to make him a subject of interest to Westerners and Japanese alike. An amazing number of the more than a dozen works he published on Japan remain in print, and books dealing with his life and work continue to appear. The Hearn Museum at Matsue is a popular point of interest for visitors to Japan willing to move beyond the standard tourist places, and there is a monument to his memory as well in the small city of Yaizu on the eastern side of Honshu where he spent his summer vacations during his later years. In addition to his importance as an early observer and interpreter of Japanese life and culture, Hearn's experience also serves in a larger sense as a kind of symbol for foreigners generally trying to make a place for themselves in Japan. Like Will Adams three centuries earlier, Hearn attempted to make Japan his home. Unlike Adams, however-- the quintessential pragmatist who came largely by accident, had little choice about

---

[8]Interestingly, he was replaced in the position by the great, early 20th century Japanese novelist Natsume Soseki (1867-1916).

staying, and seems to have accepted things pretty much as he found them-- Hearn's romantic background and restless spirit brought him to Japan initially on a kind of quixotic quest for cultural perfection and a lost world of childhood innocence. Following a euphoric first encounter, subsequent experience brought disillusionment, but the task he had set for himself (as well as for Japan) was in the end an impossible one. Perhaps no outsider can ever fully become a part of another culture, but the problem is especially difficult in a country as insular and culturally-homogeneous as Japan. It was the supreme irony in the life of this essentially 'homeless' traveler that he ultimately chose this land as the place to attempt to make a home. His failure to fully achieve this thus continues to give his life a special significance for others of similar outlook who attempt to project too much of themselves into their own 'land of dreams.'[9]

[AUTHOR'S NOTE: Hearn and the legend of Urashima]

Most contemporary commentators on Hearn take note of his great personal attachment to the Japanese legend of Urashima.[10] In this famous folktale a young boy, Urashima, is out at sea fishing. He sails far from his home and because of an act of kindness (he spares the life of a giant sea turtle) is visited by the daughter of the God of the Sea who invites him to come and live with her in a land "where summer never dies." He goes with her and spends three happy years there. But at last he grows lonely and asks to be allowed to return to his old home to visit his aging parents. With great sadness she lets him go, giving him before he leaves a small box to take with him which he promises never to open. When he returns to his home, however, he discovers that his parents have died and that everything there has changed, and in a moment of despair he opens the box. As soon as he does so a white vapor escapes from it and heads out over the sea, and he knows that he will never be able to return to the enchanted land and the Sea God's beautiful daughter. Then he too begins to change, and in a instant his body withers and becomes old, and he dies.

---

[9]See, for example, Michael Shapiro's use of Hearn in his own recent account of his experiences and those of other foreigners in Japan, in *Japan: In the Land of the Brokenhearted* (N.Y.: Holt, 1989).
[10]See Cott, *op. cit.*, pp.4-5; Carl Dawson, *Lafacdio Hearn and the Vision of Japan* (Baltimore: The Johns Hopkins Press, 1992), pp. 27-8.

Hearn's fondness for this ancient tale-- he produced his own version of it in *Out of the East* published in 1895-- can, of course, be taken on a number of different levels. On one level it can be seen as a metaphor for his own lost childhood and the memory of the mother who deserted him, and on another for his eventual disillusionment with all of the places, including Japan, where he attempted to search for and recover this lost past. On yet another level it becomes a metaphor for the human condition itself, and the process by which all human beings age and look backward to a time of lost innocence. Whatever interpretation one chooses, there is little question concerning the importance of this story for Hearn. I include it here as one more point of entry into the mind of this interesting but troubled individual. For further insights into the man and his work see the biographical and critical studies cited in the footnotes, and, of course his own works, the principal ones which relate to Japan being listed in the bibliography below.

HEARN'S MAJOR WORKS DEALING WITH JAPAN

Glimpses of Unfamiliar Japan (1894)
Out of the East: Reveries and Studies in New Japan (1895)
Kokoro: Hints and Echoes of Japanese Inner life (1896)
Gleanings in Buddha-Fields: Studies of Hand and Soul in the Far East
       (1897)
Exotics and Retrospectives (1898)
Japanese Fairy Tales, 5 vols. (1898-1922)
In Ghostly Japan (1899)
Shadowings (1900)
A Japanese Miscellany (1901)
Kotto: Being Japanese Curios, with Sundry Cobwebs (1902)
Kwaidan: Stories and Studies of Strange Things (1904)
Japan: An Attempt at Interpretation (1904)
The Romance of the Milky Way, and Other Studies and Stories (1905)

STUDY/DISCUSSION QUESTIONS FOR LAFCADIO HEARN

1. In what ways do the events of Hearn's life prior to arriving in Japan help explain his initial response to the country? What were the major aspects of Japanese culture which attracted him at that stage?

2. What were the key factors leading to his eventual disillusionment with Japan?

3. Both Lafcadio Hearn and Will Adams took Japanese wives and attempted to make Japan their home. What parallels, if any, do you see in their subsequent experiences? How do you think the very different backgrounds and temperaments of these two individuals conditioned the degree to which they were able to find happiness in Japan?

4. What are some of the possible interpretations of the Japanese legend of Urashima which help to explain Hearn's great fondness for it?

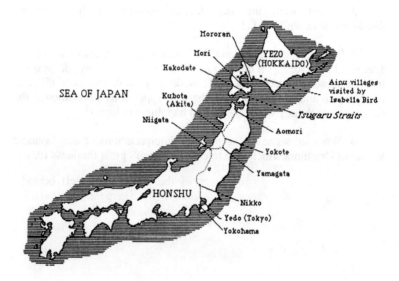

Mororan

Mori

Hakodate

YEZO
(HOKKAIDO)

Ainu villages
visited by
Isabella Bird

SEA OF JAPAN

Kubota
(Akita)

Niigata

Tsugaru Straits

Aomori

Yokote

Yamagata

HONSHU

Nikko

Yedo (Tokyo)

Yokohama

Chapter 7

Isabella Bird
(1831-1904)

19th Century Traveler and Author

Among the many travelers to Japan in the period following the
Meiji Restoration and the reopening of the country who left behind
written accounts of their experiences, was a truly remarkable woman,
Isabella Bird. Unlike Lafcadio Hearn, Bird spent less than a year in the
country, but the work she produced on her travels stands as one of the
most interesting and lasting of these late 19th century narratives.

Isabella Bird was born in 1831 in Tattenhall, Cheshire, England,
the daughter of a Protestant clergyman. In her mid-twenties she was
diagnosed with a spinal ailment, and in 1854, at the suggestion of her
physician, traveled to Canada and the U.S. as a means of improving her
health. This experience awakened a lifelong interest in travel, and also
led to the beginnings of her career as a writer when she later published
two books on her experiences, *The Englishwoman in America (1856)*
and *Aspects of Religion in the United States* (1859). During the 1860's
she lived in Edinburgh with her mother and younger sister following
the death of her father, and confined her travels and writings to that
general locale. In the early 1870's, however, again plagued by health
problems-- the 20th century reader reading between the lines here can
see at work the mechanism by which an unconventional woman in a
highly conventional time and place found the means of justifying her
somewhat unorthodox behavior and interests-- she once again set out

48   Japan Encountered

on a more extended journey, this time to Australia and the Hawaiian
Islands. Once again a book followed these experiences, eventually
published as *Six Months in the Sandwich Islands* in 1875, and in the
meantime (in 1873) she had embarked on another trip to North
America, this time to the Rocky Mountain region. As the destinations
of these later trips suggest, her travels had become increasingly
adventurous. In her Hawaii narrative she included an account of her
climb to the top of Mauna Loa, the world's largest volcano, and in the
Rocky Mountains, in the words of one biographer, "she [rode] hundreds
of miles on horseback through empty tracts of beautiful, untamed,
scarcely charted country, stayed in primitive shacks, [ate] basic food--
and had never felt fitter in her life before."[1] It was this growing interest
in the new and untried which paved the way for her 1878 trip to Japan.

Later citing the same "health" problems which had provided the
rationale for her earlier trips,[2] she set out for Japan, arriving in
Yokohama in May of 1878. Her purpose in coming was not merely to
write another "Book on Japan," but rather the hope of being able "to
contribute something to the sum of knowledge of the present condition
of the country." To this end she had planned a journey into the northern
part of Honshu and further north yet to the island of Yezo (Hokkaido),
following a route "never... traversed in its entirety by any European."[3]
After a period of a little over two weeks in Yokohama and Yedo
(Tokyo), spent convincing the local authorities, both Japanese and
British, of the advisability of her undertaking,[4] and equipping herself for

---

[1]Pat Barr, "Introduction" to Isabella L. Bird, *Unbeaten Tracks in Japan*
(Boston: Beacon Press, 1987), p. xviii. The second North American trip
also resulted in a book, *A Lady's Life in the Rocky Mountains*, published in
1879.
[2]The "Preface" to her Japan book begins: "Having been recommended to
leave home, in April 1878, in order to recruit my health by means which
had proved serviceable before, I decided to visit Japan..." (*Unbeaten
Tracks...*, p. 1). Although she makes periodic references to back pain,
sometimes of a rather severe character, throughout her narrative, it scarcely
seems to have deterred her from the rigorous plan of her undertaking.
[3]*Ibid.*
[4]Although many supported her project, some advised against it. Among the
latter was the acting British consul Mr. Wilkerson, who thought her "plan
for travelling in the interior...rather too ambitious," and Dr. Hepburn, the
eminent linguist and missionary, who expressed considerable doubt that
she would "get through to the Tsugaru Strait" (*Ibid.*, pp. 11, 22). Given
Bird's personality, these well-intentioned warnings undoubtedly added to
her determination to proceed with her plan.

the journey-- the latter included the hiring of an interpreter, a young Japanese named Ito who remained with her throughout her Japan adventure--she left the area of the foreign settlements and headed north in a convoy consisting of three *kurumas* (Japanese rickshaws). She proceeded first to Nikko, the burial place of Tokugawa Ieyasu, the founder of the Tokugawa *bakufu*, in its beautiful, forested setting deep in the mountains north of the capital. Her letters written during this portion of the trip-- all of Bird's early writings were in the form of letters to her younger sister, Henrietta, back in Britain-- offer a vivid contrast between the difficulties of travel (especially the primitive conditions, lack of privacy and armies of fleas found in Japanese wayside inns *(yadoya)*, and the great natural beauty of the Nikko region. (She had been warned about the fleas in particular on several occasions prior to setting out on her journey, and had been given a variety of advice on how to deal with them ranging from sleeping "in a bag drawn tightly round my throat" to smearing "the skin all over with carbolic oil." The stark reality of this problem was quickly encountered, as she laments to her sister in one letter-- "I tried to write to you, but fleas and mosquitoes prevented it."[5]) From Nikko, having switched to horseback as the primary mode of travel, she and her small party comprised of Ito and varying numbers of Japanese engaged at various points along the way proceeded north once again, into wild and unfamiliar country, far off the common path of tourists even in modern times.

A glance at the map at the beginning of the chapter shows a reasonably accurate approximation of the route taken-- to Niigata on the Japan Sea, inland again and northward through the towns of Yamagata and Yokote to Kubota (now the modern city of Akita), also located on the sea, and then the final leg of the journey, inland once again, to Aomori at the northern end of Honshu. Bird's record of the hardships as well as the great natural beauty of the route continues in her letters, along with numerous observations and descriptions of the local people and manner of life encountered along the way. Of particular note in this latter regard are her thoughts on the conditions of the women she finds in this interior region of Japan. Overall she finds their lot an unhappy one. At one point, while still in the vicinity of Nikko, she writes that the "girls [here] marry at sixteen, and shortly these comely, rosy, wholesome-looking creatures pass into haggard, middle-aged women with vacant faces, owing to the blackening of the teeth [an age-old

[5]*Ibid.*, pp. 22, 44. The lack of privacy experienced at one local inn, with people peering through the *fusuma* (sliding doors) of her room throughout the night (p. 44), is also noted as a source of annoyance.

custom in Japan] and removal of the eyebrows, which, if they do not follow betrothal, are resorted to on the birth of the first child." Later, at a location further north, she writes again that "[s]ome of the younger women [at that spot] might have been comely, if soap and water had been plentifully applied to their faces; but soap is not used, and such washing as the garments get is only the rubbing [of] them a little with sand in a running stream." Interestingly, even the women of the Ainu (the indigenous peoples of Hokkaido) who she encounters later on, "look cheerful, and even merry when they smile, and are not like the Japanese, prematurely old." She attributes this to the fact that the houses of these northerners "are well ventilated, and the use of charcoal is unknown," although one supposes part of it as well is the lack of the tooth blackening custom, which Bird found so appalling during the earlier portion of her journey.[6] Traveling sometimes by horseback, sometimes by *kuruma,* and occasionally by boat down inland rivers, Bird and Ito finally arrived at Aomori in the early part of August, and from there embarked on the final leg of the journey, to the northern island of Yezo.

Crossing the Tsugaru Straits by boat to the port city of Hakodate, Bird and Ito then proceeded across the tip of Hokkaido's southern peninsula to the town of Mori, traveling from there by boat once again to Mororan on the island's long, southern coast. From there, chiefly by horseback, she undertook to visit a number of Ainu villages--Shiraoi, Biratori, Mombets, Usu, Lebunge, Oshamambe-- located in that area, leaving behind in her writings a detailed and valuable account of Ainu life and culture.[7] She returned to Hakodate in mid-September, and from there completed her return trip to Yedo by ship. Altogether, her 3-month journey overland through the back country and northern wilderness of Japan had encompassed an amazing 1,400 miles!

Bird left Japan in December of 1878 and never returned. Her account of her experiences, *Unbeaten Tracks in Japan,* was published in 1880. In the years that followed, her travels took her to Singapore and the Malay States, Persia and Kurdistan, Tibet, Korea and China, and resulted in five more books. In between her Japan journey and these later trips she managed to include a five-year (1881-1886) marriage to one Dr. Bishop (so that her later works are published under that last

---

[6]*Ibid.,* pp. 79, 88, 275.
[7]Among the more interesting are her account (in vivid contrast to her earlier quoted statement about the condition of Ainu women) of the painful and deforming practice of tattooing young girls (pp. 264ff.), and her discussion of the famous Ainu cult of bear worship (pp. 280ff.).

name). On her last journey, to Morocco at the age of seventy, she toured that region on a black stallion given to her by the sultan of the country. She died tranquilly at home in Scotland in 1904.

[AUTHOR'S NOTE: Other women of the period]

Isabella Bird would have been an extraordinary person in any age. A more typical account of a Western woman's experiences in Japan in the late 19th century can be found in the works of Mary C. Fraser (1851-1922). The daughter of the American sculptor, Thomas Crawford, and older sister of the novelist Francis Marion Crawford, Mary Crawford married Hugh Fraser, a British diplomat, in 1874, and accompanied him to Tokyo when he was appointed ambassador to Japan in 1889 (she had previously been with him at posts in China, Vienna and Chile). In her two works, *A Diplomatist's Wife in Japan: Letters from Home to Home* (1899) and *Further Reminiscences of a Diplomatist's Wife* (1912), she records the more conventional lifestyle of a woman of her time and station. An excellent writer and woman of wide-ranging interests, she also includes general comments on a vast variety of subjects relating to Japan in her works.[8]

---

[8]Pat Barr includes brief discussions of the experiences of both Bird and Fraser in her work *The Deer Cry Pavilion; A Story of Westerners in Japan 1868-1905* (London: Penguin Books, 1988), pp. 83-99 and 150-7 respectively.

STUDY/DISCUSSION QUESTIONS FOR
ISABELLA BIRD

1. In what ways did Isabella Bird depart from the traditional lifestyle and role of women in the Victorian Age? What excuse did she use to justify her unorthodox pursuits and interests? What do you think may have been the underlying motivation for her many journeys?

2. What was the state of Japanese development at the time (the late 1870's) of Bird's trip to northern Japan? What factors made her trip especially difficult? Who were the Ainu peoples that Bird visited in Yezo (modern day Hokkaido)?

3. What were Bird's views of the women she encountered during her trip through the northern interior of Japan? How accurate do you think her observations were, and to what extent do you think her own cultural biases (against the blackening of teeth, for example) may have entered into her judgements?

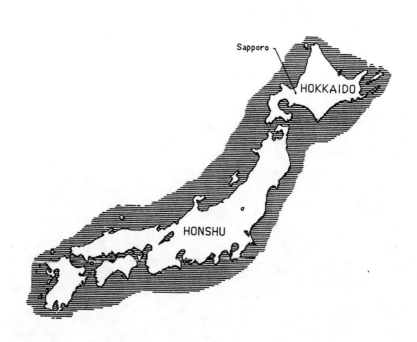

Chapter 8

William Smith Clark
(1826-1886)

Teacher and Role Model from the West

In addition to the Western travelers and observers who came to
view Japan in the second half of the 19th century, there was also
another class of individuals who entered the country in relatively large
numbers during this period. These were the Western advisors, recruited
by the Japanese government, to assist in the process of modernization.
One of the earliest and best known of these individuals was William
Smith Clark.

Born in Ashfield, Massachusetts in 1826, Clark was educated at
Amherst College in Massachusetts and at Georgia Augusta University
in Gottingen, Germany. After receiving his Ph.D. degree in chemistry
from the latter institution in 1852, he returned to Amherst as a faculty
member and taught there for the next fifteen years, interrupted only by
two years of military service (1861-1863) during the Civil War. In
1867 he left Amherst to become the first president of the Massachusetts
Agricultural College, a newly-formed state agricultural college which he
had helped to found. It was while serving in this position that he was
recruited by the Japanese government, in 1876, to come to Japan to
help in the founding of a new agricultural college in the then northern
Japanese colony of Hokkaido.[1]

---

[1]Hokkaido at that time had only recently been opened up for development.

Clark arrived at Sapporo, the site of the new college, in July of 1876 on a one-year leave from his home institution. The new college was opened two weeks later with Clark serving as its first dean and president. During the months ahead he helped in the planning of the school's curriculum, taught classes, and served as a technical advisor to the local government on the subject of agricultural development. In this latter capacity he assisted in the introduction of new crops and agricultural techniques, and wrote numerous reports on the agricultural potential of the region.

In addition to his scientific expertise and interests, Clark was also a devout Christian and attempted to promote Christianity in the college by urging his students to sign a "Covenant of Believers in Jesus," in anticipation of their eventual conversion to the faith. Many apparently did convert, although the overall success of Christianity in Japan during this period was rather limited. Of greater significance to his students seems to have been the model he offered of the knowledgeable and enterprising Westerner. Leaving Sapporo in the spring of 1877, he supposedly turned in his saddle as he rode off and left them with the following admonition-- *"Boys, be ambitious!"* This brief saying remains familiar to nearly every Japanese down to the present day, and is inscribed on a bust of Clark which stands at the front of Clark Hall on the agricultural section of what is now Hokkaido University.

Clark, who died in 1881 and never returned to Japan, thus stands as a brief but important example of two key influences effecting Japan in the late 19th century. These were: 1) the technological superiority of the West (and the conscious effort of those in charge of Japan's development to learn from it, as well as to inculcate its associated values), and 2) the reintroduction of Christianity (and its only modest success in the country during this later period). Both directions would continue to be of considerable importance in the years ahead.[2]

Its geographical situation and agricultural potential were quite different from that of the rest of the country, and more similar in many ways to those of Clark's home region in the U.S.

[2]One can see evidence of the former in the recruitment of Frank Lloyd Wright for the design of the Imperial Hotel in Tokyo in the early years of the 20th century (see following chapter)-- although as that discussion suggests, the Japanese influence *on* Wright was at least as important as was *his* influence upon Japan. Perhaps a better example exists in the case of W. Edward Deming, an American expert on statistical quality control, who was invited to Japan in the period following World War II to lecture on his ideas. Deming's methods were then put into practice by the Japanese in the form of quality control circles, an idea which contributed significantly to

STUDY/DISCUSSION QUESTIONS FOR
WILLIAM SMITH CLARK

1. For what reasons was Clark selected by the Japanese government to assist in the opening of the new agricultural college in Hokkaido?

2. In what ways did Clark serve as a role model for his students? Which American values or attributes did Clark come to symbolize for the Japanese?

3. Why do you think Christianity has grown so slowly in Japan in the recent era?

the revitalization of Japanese industry in the postwar period but has gained attention only recently in the U.S. The slow growth of Christianity is evidenced by the fact that even at the present time only about 1 million of Japan's 124 million people are Christian.

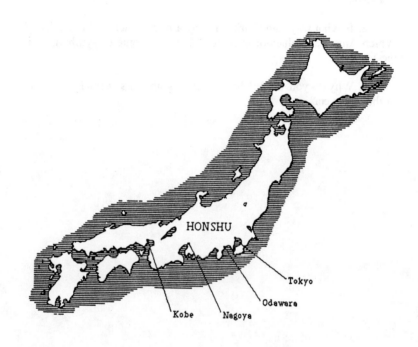

HONSHU

Tokyo

Odawara

Kobe   Nagoya

Chapter 9

Frank Lloyd Wright
(1867-1959)

A Case Study in Cross-cultural Influence

Frank Lloyd Wright, one of the great figures in 20th century architecture, had a long and important connection with Japan. Born in Richland Center, Wisconsin in 1867, Wright spent his formative years under the dual influences of his schoolteacher mother (who he claimed had chosen architecture for him as his life's work before he was born) and a life lived close to nature on the farm of an uncle where he frequently spent his summers. In his late teens he briefly attended the University of Wisconsin at Madison, studying engineering and literature, but in 1887, at the age of 20, was drawn to Chicago where the great buildings of the period were being created by such figures in American architecture as J. W. Silsbee, Daniel Burnham and Louis Sullivan. Working first for Silsbee, and then shifting in 1888 to the famous firm of Adler and Sullivan, Wright imbibed at first hand the ideas that were to give birth to modern architecture. It was also in Chicago, at the Columbian Exposition of 1893, that the Japanese influence may first have entered Wright's work and thinking.

At that famous fair, created to celebrate the 400th anniversary of Columbus' arrival in the New World, the Japanese contributed a building modeled after the Ho-o-do (or Phoenix Hall) of an 11th century Buddhist temple (Byodoin) near Kyoto. Standing on a small wooded island in the Exposition site's main lagoon, the building, with its

traditional Japanese form, stood in sharp contrast to the majority of the
fair buildings which were done in the then-popular Neo-Classical style
with its profusion of "columns, entablatures, arches, vaults and
domes."[1] It was this building, along with a collection of Japanese
woodblock prints (ukiyo-e) also on display at the Exposition, which
some commentators believe first fired the imagination of Wright and
his contemporaries, and brought the Japanese line of influence into their
work.[2] By the early 1900's Wright had become a collector of Japanese
prints-- a life-long interest upon which he later published a book[3]-- and,
in a deeper sense, according to these same authors, the Japanese
aesthetic was combining with various indigenous "American"
influences to give birth to the "Prairie school," or what Wright was in
the process of defining as "organic architecture."[4]

One writer (Lancaster) traces the presence of the Japanese
influence in Wright's work from at least 1895 and a house he designed
in that year for Chauncey Williams in Lake Forest, Illinois. From this
work, which demonstrates, in that author's words, "a Japanese
picturesqueness," Wright moved to a more substantial use of Japanese
elements in houses designed in 1900 and 1901.[5] By the early years of
the century Wright's seminal role in the development of the "Prairie
style" in domestic architecture, manifesting the elements of simplicity
and the integration of the design into the natural landscape (both

---

[1] Clay Lancaster, The Japanese Influence in America (New York: Abbeville
Press, 1983), p. 76.
[2] See Lancaster, chapter 9. An earlier vogue for things Japanese had occurred
as a result of a Japanese exhibit at the Centennial Exposition in
Philadelphia in 1876 but with nothing like the same degree of depth or
profundity (see same source, chapters 5 and 6).
[3] The Japanese Print (1912). See also Wright's An Autobiography (New
York: Horizon Press, 1977), pp. 550-7 for an account of some of his
experiences as a print collector.
[4] For brief discussions of Wright's architectural ideas see Corinne J. Naden,
Frank Lloyd Wright: The Rebel Architect (New York: Franklin Watts,
1968), pp. 119-24, or An Autobiography, pp. 168-73. It should be noted
that Wright probably used the term "organic" in this connection for the
first time in 1894, in a talk entitled "The Architect and the Machine." [The
author wishes to thank Ms. Margo Stipe of The Frank Lloyd Wright
Archives for providing this latter reference, as well as for her other helpful
suggestions on this chapter.]
[5] The Bradley and Hickox houses in Kankakee, Illinois, and Penwern, a
house designed for Fred B. Jones in Delevan Lake, Wisconsin (Lancaster,
op. cit., pp. 85, 86-7).

elements strongly represented in the Japanese tradition), was well underway, with a corresponding growth in his own reputation and degree of financial success. In 1905, in the midst of these early achievements, he made his first trip to Japan. The chief purposes of the journey involved his pursuit of Japanese prints and the need to rest after a period of intense work, but once having arrived in the country the deeper, esthetic dimensions of Japanese art and architecture took hold of him. As he was later to write, "Japanese art, I found, really did have organic character, was nearer to the earth and a more indigenous product of native conditions of life and work therefore more nearly 'modern' as I saw it, than any European civilization alive or dead."[6]

In the period following his return to the U.S., Wright's work continued to expand and develop. In 1906, Unity Church in Oak Park, Illinois, one of his most striking early nonresidential designs (and one demonstrating a strong Japanese influence), was completed.[7] He continued to design homes in the "Prairie style," and in 1911 he began work on his own house, which also contained strong Japanese elements-- Taliesin in Spring Green, Wisconsin. At the same time, however, his personal life was taking a disastrous turn. By the early years of the century his marriage to Catherine Tobin, his first wife who he had married in 1890 and by whom he had fathered six children, was faltering, and around that time he began a relationship with Mamah Cheney, the wife of one of his clients. This relationship lasted until her tragic death in 1914. In August of that year she and six other individuals, including her two children who were visiting at the time, were murdered by a mentally-deranged house servant at Taliesin, who subsequently burned down the house as well. Wright, who was in Chicago at the time of the incident, was devastated by the loss. This event, along with the adverse publicity which had been mounting as a result of his relationship with Cheney while he was still married to his first wife (who had refused to give him a divorce), underlay his decision the following year to return to Japan, this time to design and supervise the building of what was to be one of his most celebrated works, the Imperial Hotel in Tokyo.

---

[6]*An Autobiography* (1932 edition), reprinted in *Frank Lloyd Wright Collected Writings*, Vol. 2 (New York: Rizzoli, 1992), pp. 243-4. (Used with permission of The Frank Lloyd Wright Foundation.)
[7]William H. Jordy, in Volume 5 of *American Buildings and Their Architects: The Impact of European Modernism in the 20th Century* (New York: Oxford University Press, 1972), pp. 303-4, discusses specifically the Japanese influence on the Unity Church design.

The work on the Imperial Hotel, which according to his account was offered to him by a group of individuals from Japan who had been touring the world in search of an architectural style which appealed to them, kept Wright in Japan for the better part of the next six years and constituted his most extended period of exposure to Japanese life and culture. In addition, these years provide an interesting case study in cross-cultural influence-- in the continuing influence of Japan on Wright's own work, and in the opportunity the work provided *him* for the application of American ingenuity and engineering skills, especially in regard to that most serious of Japanese structural challenges, the earthquake.

In an extended passage in his later autobiography, reminiscent at times of Hearn's "My First Day in the Orient"-- he even refers at one point to "old Japan" (along with "old Germany") as the dual "*lands of* [his] *dreams*" (emphasis my own)-- Wright clearly displays the continuing importance of Japan as a source of artistic inspiration.[8] "Becoming more closely acquainted with things Japanese," he writes during the course of this adulation, "I saw the native home in Japan as supreme study in elimination-- not only of dirt but the elimination, too, of the insignificant."[9] It was this dictum of "the elimination... of the insignificant"-- translated into the even more basic term "simplicity"-- which was, of course, a central tenet of Wright's architectural philosophy and played a key role in the development of modern architecture as well. In a more specific sense, Wright, in his own words, became "fascinated"[10] with Japanese domestic design and provided an extended discussion of the subject in this same section of the autobiography, thus further highlighting its importance as a part of his overall development during this period.

On the other side of the equation, the matter of designing an earthquake-proof structure (an earlier hotel on the same site had been destroyed by just such an occurrence), presented Wright with a problem of considerable technical difficulty. In another section of the autobiography[11] he explains the innovations undertaken to create a

---

[8]The section, comprised of two parts, "A Song of Heaven" and "Yedo," begins on p. 218 (1977 ed.). The "old Japan" reference is on the preceding page. (Used with permission of The Frank Lloyd Wright Foundation.)
[9]*An Autobiography* (1932 ed.), p. 245. (Used with permission of The Frank Lloyd Wright Foundation.)
[10]*Ibid.*
[11]"Building Against Doomsday (Why the Great Earthquake Did Not Destroy the Imperial Hotel)," *An Autobigraphy* (1977 ed.), pp. 236ff.

design to withstand this frequent Japanese calamity. Since the earth beneath the structure was actually, in Wright's words, "liquid mud," with a layer of approximately eight feet of soil above it, the plan hit upon was to "float" the foundation *on* the mud rather than to attempt to anchor it firmly beneath it (which would have required driving piles to a depth of sixty or seventy feet). In addition, the building was designed as a series of jointed sections to prevent cracking, and the floors constructed as cantilevered slabs of concrete stretching out from a central core instead of resting upon the walls in the conventional manner. Needless-to-say, Wright's design was unprecedented and highly-controversial, but within a month of the building's completion (and on the very day of the official opening ceremonies) it was put to the supreme test in the Great Kanto Earthquake of September 1, 1923, which destroyed a large portion of the surrounding city. Wright's design rode out the quake, and the hotel served as a temporary shelter for hundreds of people who had lost their homes in the disaster. In addition to the hotel's innovative foundation and structural design, its exterior design and interior decor offered, in the eyes of most, a unique and unusual blending of Wright's architectural ideas with traditional Japanese elements. The Imperial Hotel remained a part of the Tokyo landscape until 1967, when, despite considerable international protest, it was torn down. A portion of the building, however, was preserved and reassembled at Meiji Mura, a historical park near Nagoya, where it still stands as at least a reminder of its former splendor and elegance.

During Wright's close to six years in Japan he was also involved in several other Japanese commissions, among them: a hotel in Odawara, several houses, and, with one of his Japanese associates, Endo Arata, the Jiyu Gakuen School in 1921.[12] After returning to the U.S. in 1922, the Japanese influence in his work continued to be an important one. Lancaster argues convincingly for the role of Japanese ideas in "Falling Water," Wright's famous house built over a waterfall in 1936, as well as in other residential designs from approximately the same period, and in the Johnson Wax Tower completed in 1939.[13] In addition, his role in influencing a younger generation of architects, such as Antonin Raymond (who spent most of his career in Japan) and

---

[12]Wright's vogue in Japan coincided with a period of great interest generally in the country for things relating to the West, as it underwent its own version of the "Jazz Age" and the "Roaring 20's." For more on Wright's other Japanese commissions see Masami Tanigawa, "Wright's Little-Known Japanese Projects," in the *Frank Lloyd Wright Quarterly*, Vol. 6, No.2 (Spring 1995), pp. 16-20.

[13]Lancaster, *op. cit.,* pp. 160-5, 220.

Richard Neutra (who also displayed strong connections with Japan in
his work), is also significant.

When the U.S. declared war on Japan in December of 1941,
Wright, who was well-known for his pacifist views, spoke out
publically in the attempt to offer a counter perspective on Japan's
policies. While his review of U.S.-Japanese relations in the years
following Perry and his thoughts on Japan's portrayal of itself as
'liberator' and 'emancipator' in Asia during this period are often rather
naive, they nonetheless contain elements of historical truth, and are no
less informed in their way than were the thoughts of many American
policymakers (see Chapter 11) during the period.[14]

In the end, Wright's relationship with Japan was both long and
complex. As with the work of any genius, controversies continue to
rage over his work, and the question of the overall importance of Japan
in it is no exception; just as there are those who argue for the centrality
of this influence, there are others who question the degree to which
Wright *ever* succeeded in bringing at least the *true* essence of Japan into
it.[15] Even Wright himself seems to have attempted on some occasions
to disavow the Japanese line of influence.[16] Whatever conclusions one
reaches on these matters, however, it is difficult to deny Wright's own
words, written and spoken on numerous occasions over the years, on
the subject. Writing once again in his autobiography on the role of the
Japanese print (and by extension, one can argue, of the larger Japanese
esthetic) in his work, he states:

> The print is more autobiographical than you may imagine. If
> Japanese prints were to be deducted from my education I don't
> know what direction the whole might have taken.

---

[14]See *An Autobiography* (1977 ed.), pp. 547-50, 557-61. The references to
liberation and emancipation are on p. 560.

[15]See, for example, the comments by Antonin Raymond, who served as
Wright's chief assistant in the early stages of the design of the Imperial
Hotel, to the effect that Wright's "design had nothing in common with
Japan, its climate, its traditions, its people and its culture," and was
instead, first and foremost, "the expression of his own personal
imaginings" (quoted in John Tran, "So Wrong Frank Lloyd Wright," *Kansai
Time Out*, August 1993, p. 12).

[16]See, for example, *Kodansha Encyclopedia of Japan* (Tokyo: Kodansha,
1983), vol. 12, p. 279, or Naden, *op. cit.*, p. 44. "Frank Lloyd Wright and
Japan," in the *Frank Lloyd Wright Quarterly*, Vol. 6, No. 2 (Spring 1995),
pp. 3-7, provides a good summary of Wright's often contradictory
statements on this subject.

The gospel of elimination preached by the print came
home to me in architecture as it came home to the French
painters who developed "Cubisme" and "Futurisme."
Intrinsically it lies at the bottom of all this so-called
"modernisme." Strangely unnoticed, uncredited.[17]

Thus, whatever the specifics of the debate, it is difficult to deny the
overall importance of Frank Lloyd Wright's connection with Japan.

---

[17]*An Autobiography* (1932 ed.), pp. 250-1. (Used with permission of The
Frank Lloyd Wright Foundation.)

1. Japanese building (Ho-o-den) at the World's Columbian Exposition in Chicago in 1893 which influenced Frank Lloyd Wright and other members of the later "Prairie School." Note contrast to the more typical Exposition architecture on the far right. (Photo by John George M. Glessner. Courtesy Chicago Historical Society. G1977.0222.1186)

2. Frank Lloyd Wright, Avery Coonley House in Riverside, Ill., 1907. (Photo by Henry Fuermann. Courtesy The Frank Lloyd Wright Foundation.)

3. Interior of the Ho-o-den, 1893 (see 1. above). (Photo by C.D. Arnold. Courtesy Chicago Historical Society. ICHi-02320)

4. Frank Lloyd Wright, Unity Temple interior, Oak Park, Ill., 1906. (Courtesy, the Frank Lloyd Wright Home and Studio Foundation.)

5. A portion of Frank Lloyd Wright's Imperial Hotel (originally in Tokyo and completed in 1922) as it currently stands at Meiji Mura, outdoor historical park, near Nagoya, Japan. (Photo by the author.)

STUDY/DISCUSSION QUESTIONS FOR
FRANK LLOYD WRIGHT

1. In what ways can it be said that Japan influenced Frank Lloyd Wright? In what ways did Wright in turn influence Japan?

2. What does Wright's support for Japan at the beginning of World War II indicate regarding the personality of the man? Do these characteristics help to explain why he occasionally denied the Japanese influence in his work, despite acknowledging it in quite flowery language on numerous other occasions?

1) Nature into houses
Prairie style house
Modern technologies
2) Supports Japanese

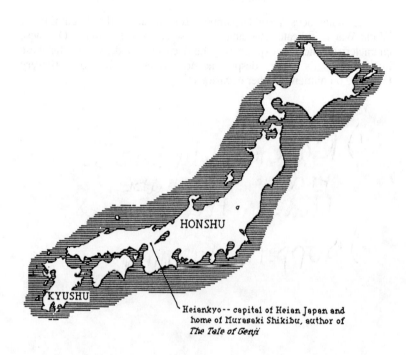

HONSHU

KYUSHU

Heiankyo-- capital of Heian Japan and
home of Murasaki Shikibu, author of
The Tale of Genji

Chapter 10

Arthur Waley
(1889-1966)

Translator of *The Tale of Genji*

Unlike the rest of the individuals surveyed in this volume so far, Arthur Waley never set foot in Japan. Still, his role in "encountering" Japan is a significant one, for his work, more than that of any other individual, served to introduce Western readers to what is often considered Japan's greatest work of literature, *The Tale of Genji*.

Born in England in 1889 into an English-Jewish family named Schloss (the family name was changed during the First World War to avoid anti-German prejudice), Waley attended Rugby and later King's College, Cambridge, where he entered the classical course. Poor eyesight forced him to quit his formal studies prior to finishing his degree, at which point he studied Chinese and Japanese on his own,[1] eventually securing a post in these fields as an assistant at the British Museum. It was while holding this position that he began his first work as a translator. His first published translations appeared under the title, *Chinese Poems,* in 1916. From that point on he produced a steady output of translations from the Chinese, including *A Hundred and*

---

[1]To anyone who has studied Chinese or Japanese this seems a rather ironic choice, given the incredible amount of close detail found in the written forms of these languages!

Seventy Chinese Poems (1918), *The Way and Its Power* (1934), *The Book of Songs* (1937), *The Analects of Confucius* (1938), *Three Ways of Thought in Ancient China* (1939), and *The Life and Times of Po Chu-i* (1949). Sandwiched in between this work he also translated a number of works of Japanese literature, including his landmark translation of the *Tale of Genji*, which was published in six volumes between 1925 and 1933.

The *Tale of Genji* (or *Genji Monogatari*) is often considered to be the greatest work of Japanese prose literature. Written in the early 11th century by a woman of the Heian court, Murasaki Shikibu, the work is a huge (over a thousand pages in translation) novel of court life, focusing on the life and times of its main character, Prince Genji. (Although the Prince himself dies approximately two-thirds of the way through the story, even the last third of the work, which details the lives of two lesser princes, exists chiefly as a contrast to Genji's earlier magnificence.) Although the work is truly a great classic, renowned for both its representation of the esthetic sensibilities of its age as well as the psychological depths of its characterization, it also embodies distinct problems of accessibility for modern readers. For one thing, its language is the language of the 11th century, written in an early mixture of *kana* (phonetic syllabaries, used at that time chiefly by women) and *kanji* (Chinese characters taken over as the "official" writing system of the country during an earlier period of cultural borrowing).[2] Most Japanese today are unable to read it in its original form and must resort to the use of translations into modern Japanese, much as modern readers of English require translations of such early English works as *The Canterbury Tales*. Related to this, the court culture and the esthetic values depicted in *The Tale of Genji* are quite difficult to relate to, especially for Western readers. The Heian period had attained a level of esthetic sensibility-- in its later stages, even at the time of the writing of *Genji*, it was in the process of slipping into decadence-- seldom surpassed in any culture, but one quite alien to modern experience.[3]

---

[2] Actually *The Tale of Genji* and the other prose works of the court women of this period made a significant contribution to the development of contemporary written Japanese, which continues, for better or worse, to use a modern form of this same combination of elements.

[3] See for example Donald Keene's essay, "Feminine Sensibility in the Heian Era," in his *Appreciations of Japanese Culture* (Tokyo: Kodansha, 1981) which discusses *The Tale of Genji* (pp. 32ff.) as the ultimate idealization of this culture, or, for a longer treatment of the subject, Ivan Morris' *The World of the Shining Prince: Court Life in Ancient Japan* (1964).

To these difficulties of translation, Waley brought a unique gift and a controversial technique. Believing strongly in the dictum that, because "so much is inevitably lost in translating Oriental literature...[,] one must give a great deal in return," he took a very loose and free approach in his translations. His method, described by Donald Keene (one of the great scholars and translators of Japanese literature who followed him), was to

> ...read a passage over until he understood its meaning; then, without looking back at the passage, [to write] out an English assimilation. He would later consult the original again. If the content of the translation was the same, he would let it pass, even if some words had been added or deleted.[4]

Although some later critics believe that Waley occasionally took too many liberties in his work, his method served to make the creations of distant and radically different cultures accessible to modern readers. Even more importantly, according to Keene, it was his translations which, more often than not, established the "tone" for the more textually-accurate translations which came later. Keene writes of *The Tale of Genji* in particular, that it "...could have been translated into a style reminiscent of *Le Morte d' Arthur*, or into the nineteenth-century Gothic favoured by Waley's predecessors in almost all their translations from classical literature."[5] Instead, Waley utilized, in the words of another commentator, the "milieu [of] an English eighteenth-century country house" as the tonal setting for his work,[6] and it is this quieter, more muted atmosphere which proves just the right touch for the re-creation of the distant Heian age. This knack for discovering the right tone or "voice" for a translation was, according to Keene, Waley's great gift. He writes that "[w]hatever new translations scholars may produce in the future, hoping to improve on the accuracy of Waley's versions, they are unlikely to alter his tone." He concludes that, in the end, all subsequent translators of Chinese and Japanese literature into English can be said to "belong to the School of Waley."[7]

---

[4]Quoted in William J. Puette, *Guide to The Tale of Genji by Murasaki Shikibu* (Tokyo: Tuttle, 1983), p. 56.
[5]Donald Keene, *Appreciations of Japanese Culture*, pp. 333-4.
[6]Original source uncertain. The quotation, a paraphrase of the original, is from J. Thomas Rimer, *A Reader's Guide to Japanese Literature* (Tokyo: Kodansha, 1991), p. 40.
[7]Keene, p. 334. Interestingly, even as great a translator as Keene found it

In 1976 another major English translation of *Genji* appeared, that of the American Edward Seidensticker. Although his work is based on a considerable amount of new scholarship and follows the original with somewhat greater care than does Waley's, Seidensticker nevertheless clearly acknowledges the role of the earlier work in his formation. He writes in the "Introduction" to his translation that-- "[Waley's translation] was my introduction to Japanese literature, and its power upon repeated readings-- I could not give their total number-- has continued to be so great that the process of preparing a new translation has felt like a sacrilege." Seidensticker concludes that "[s]ince there is no such thing as a perfect translation of a complex literary work, the more translations, one would think, the better"-- and modern readers will undoubtedly agree, some preferring the readabilty and literary flair of the Waley translation, others the greater textual accuracy of the Seidensticker.[8] (Many readers will, in fact, want to take the advice given in one recent guide of placing the two translations side by side, "comparing the work of one master translator with another," and letting both "help the sense of the buried original to come through."[9])

Waley's accomplishments as a translator were even more extraordinary given the fact that he never traveled to Japan nor learned to speak Japanese. (Despite his lack of firsthand knowledge of the Orient, experts have found his ability to evoke its atmosphere to be remarkably accurate.) Although he clearly aimed at a wide audience in his translations, his mastery of the technical side of his field was considerable. Keene writes that he "was capable of writing short scholarly articles on grammatical particles," and he also produced landmark studies on Chinese and Japanese art.[10] Despite his many accomplishments, he seems to have been a man of simple tastes and habits, totally committed to his work, and inclined to take a rather impatient view of the recognition which came to him as a result of it. (He writes on one occasion in a letter that: "...my spirits [are] weighed down by the approach of the King's annual Feast, which I have cut so

necessary to limit his work to only *one* of the two languages which Waley was proficient in, determining fairly early in his career to give up the study of Chinese, and declaring that "The most I could aspire to was to become half of Waley" (*Ibid.*, p. 332).
[8]The quotations from Seidensticker are from the "Introduction" to Murasaki Shikibu, *The Tale of Genji*, transl. by Edward G. Seidensticker, Vol. 1 (Tokyo: Tuttle, 1978), p. xiv.
[9]Rimer, *op. cit.*, p. 40.
[10]Keene, *op. cit.*, p. 334; *Kodansha Encyclopedia of Japan* (Tokyo: Kodansha, 1983), vol. 8, p. 221.

often that I felt I must face it this year.") In his last years, when poor health and the infirmities of age forced him to abandon his translating, he determined to devote his remaining energies to "refreshing his knowledge of European literature."[11]

In addition to *The Tale of Genji,* Waley also translated a number of other important works of Japanese literature. His major works in this area include: *Japanese Poetry: The Uta* (a selection of poems from the 8th century *Manyoshu* and other imperial anthologies, published in 1919), *The No Plays of Japan* (1921), *The Pillow Book of Sei Shonagon* (or *Makura no soshi* - approximately one quarter of the original, in 1928), and "The Lady Who Loved Insects" from the *Tsutsumi Chunagon Monogatari* in 1929. In each case, even though many of these translations have been superseded by fuller and more accurate versions in later years, his choice of the correct "tone" for the translations has been, in the words of Keene, "invariably definitive."[12]

[AUTHOR'S NOTE: Comparative passages from the Waley and Seidensticker translations]

Although there has been much written discussing the differences between these two famous translations of *The Tale of Genji,*[13] the following passages serve to demonstrate the basic similarities of the two works. (This comparison, of course, does not involve passages containing well-known or dramatic differences, or the larger question of sections which Waley elected to leave out, and Seidensticker, in his more complete translation, included.)

Comparison #1 - brief passage on Japanese esthetics as reflected in *shodo* (Japanese calligraphy or brush-writing)--

---

[11]Keene, pp. 336, 337. Keene's essay entitled "Arthur Waley," from which these quotations are taken, offers a warmly-affectionate portrait of the man in his later years. Another essay in the same volume ("On Translation") makes some additional mention of his work, as well as offering a number of valuable insights into the problems of translation.

[12]*Ibid.,* p. 334.

[13]See, for example, Puette, *op. cit.,* pp. 58 and 185ff. for a list of reviews and articles comparing the two translations, or Seidensticker's own comments on the subject in the "Introduction" to his work (pp. xvi-xv - full citation in footnote 8. above).

(Waley)

... So too in handwriting, we see some who aimlessly prolong their cursive strokes this way or that, and hope their flourishes will be mistaken for genius. But true penmanship preserves in every letter its balance and form, and though at first some letters may seem but half-formed, yet when we compare them with the copy-books we find that there is nothing at all amiss.

(Seidensticker)

Or let us look at calligraphy. A man without any great skill can stretch out this line and that in the cursive style and give an appearance of boldness and distinction. The man who has mastered the principles and writes with concentration may, on the other hand, have none of the eye-catching tricks; but when you take the trouble to compare the two the real thing is the real thing.

Comparison #2 - passage showing Genji revived from a lingering illness by the influence of nature--

(Waley)

... A heavy mist covered the morning sky, and even the chirruping of the mountain-birds sounded muffled and dim. Such a variety of flowers and blossoming trees (he did not know their names) grew upon the hillside that the rocks seemed to be spread with a many-coloured embroidery. Above all he marvelled at the exquisite stepping of the deer who moved across the slope, now treading daintily, now suddenly pausing; and as he watched them the last remnants of his sickness were dispelled by sheer delight. ...

(Seidensticker)

There were heavy mists in the dawn sky, and bird songs came from Genji knew not where. Flowering trees and grasses which he could not identify spread like a tapestry before him. The deer that now paused to feed by the house and now

wandered on were for him a strange and wonderful sight. He
quite forgot his illness. ... [14]

In this manner do the two translations, for the most part,
supplement and enhance each other rather than involve radical changes
or differences, and thus, too, does Seidensticker maintain the overall
"tone" of Waley's work.

---

[14]The respective quotations are from the Seidensticker translation (see
above), Vol. 1, pp. 27 and 93; and from Lady Murasaki, *The Tale of Genji*,
transl. by Arthur Waley (Garden City, NY: Doubleday, 1955), pp. 30-1 and
120.

STUDY/DISCUSSION QUESTIONS FOR
ARTHUR WALEY

1. What is *The Tale of Genji?* When was it written? By whom? What are some of the problems involved in translating it for modern readers?

2. What methods did Arthur Waley utilize in his translation of *Genji?*

3. What was perhaps Waley's most important contribution as one of the earliest and most prolific translators of Oriental literature into English?

--Historical Interlude--

Parallels and Conflicts: Backgrounds of the War Between the U.S. and Japan

A review of the major events leading to the war between the U.S. and Japan (1941-1945) reveals a pattern of historical parallels intermingled with vivid contrasts and continuing points of conflict commencing almost ninety years before the onset of the war.

Beginning with Commodore Perry's arrival in Tokyo Bay in the 1850's, Japan was catapulted headlong into the modern world at precisely the same time that the U.S., too, was undergoing the forces of modernization. Both countries experienced periods of severe internal unrest as a test of their new directions-- the United States in the U.S. Civil War *(1861-5), Japan in the internal strife leading to the* Meiji Restoration *(1868) and in the later challenge of the* Satsuma Rebellion *(1877). Both likewise flexed their muscles on the international scene as emerging world powers at almost precisely the same time, the Japanese in the* Sino-Japanese War *of 1894-5 and the U.S. in the* Spanish-American War *three years later, and it was this period as well which saw the growing competition of the two nations in the Pacific as the U.S. assumed control over the Philippines, Guam and Hawaii, and Japan acquired Taiwan and began its attempt to establish a foothold in China.*

In the early years of the new century both the parallels as well as the points of conflict continued. In the latter area, racial prejudice in the U.S., which led to the placing of strict limits on Japanese immigration at a time when unrestricted immigration was allowed from European countries (the so-called "Gentlemen's Agreement" of 1907), created a negative tone in U.S.-Japanese relations, while Japanese opportunism and attempts at territorial gain at the time of the First World War, *when the laws governing international behavior were changing from the 'survival of the fittest' doctrine of Charles Darwin to the 'universalism' of Woodrow Wilson, also produced tensions.*

Later, in the 1920's, both countries experienced their own versions of the "Jazz Age" and dramatic social change, but by the early 1930's both were likewise experiencing the devastating effects of worldwide economic depression and seeking, each in its own way, to find methods of dealing with it. The U.S., with the arrival of Franklin Roosevelt and the New Deal in 1933, searched for a solution through unprecedented

80 Japan Encountered

government intervention in its domestic economy, while Japan embarked on a course of militarism and international aggression, beginning with the military occupation of Manchuria in 1931 and the later war with China (commencing in 1937), which would take it eventually into the cataclysm of the Pacific War.

Against this backdrop, the careers of the following two men-- Joseph Grew, American Ambassador to Japan during the critical prewar years, and Douglas MacArthur, key strategist of Japan's defeat and head of the postwar Occupation-- were acted out.

(For a fuller chronology of the events from the arrival of Perry in 1853 to the Japanese attack on Pearl Harbor in December of 1941, see Appendix II *at the end of this volume.)*

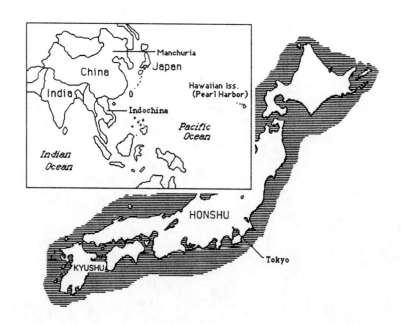

Manchuria

China

Japan

India

Hawaiian Iss.
(Pearl Harbor)

Indochina

Pacific
Ocean

Indian
Ocean

HONSHU

KYUSHU

Tokyo

Chapter 11

Joseph Grew
(1880-1965)

Struggling Against the Flow of History

The road leading to the Japanese attack on Pearl Harbor and the U.S. entry into the Pacific War was a long and tortuous one, with numerous choices on both sides which might have led to a different result. Looking back over this period of history today one tends to see only the inexorable drift toward disaster, but to those embroiled in the day-to-day life of those times it did not always appear so hopeless. One of these individuals who struggled valiantly against the flow of events, was Joseph C. Grew, U.S. Ambassador to Japan from 1932 to 1942. Grew arrived in Japan less than a year after the "Manchurian Incident" marked the beginning of Japan's aggression in Asia and only a month after a coup attempt (the "5-15 Incident" in May of 1932) severely challenged democratic government in Japan and added significantly to the power of the military.[1] During the years which followed, he struggled without success to avert the catastrophe of war with the U.S.

Few individuals of his day would have been considered better prepared for the assignment. Born in Boston in 1880, Grew was educated at Groton and Harvard, where he graduated two years ahead of Franklin Roosevelt, the man whose policies he was to represent to the

---

[1]For a detailed chronology of the events discussed in this chapter see Appendix II.

Japanese. After college he travelled extensively in the Far East, to India, Malaya and other parts of Southeast Asia, later writing a book, *Sport and Travel in the Far East*, detailing his experiences. The book was apparently read by President Theodore Roosevelt, who appointed Grew to his first diplomatic assignment in Cairo in 1904. In the years prior to arriving in Japan he had held diplomatic posts in Mexico, Russia, Austria-Hungary, Germany (in the period just before the U.S. entry into the First World War), Vienna, Denmark, Switzerland and Turkey, in addition to serving as a member of the U.S. negotiating team at the Paris Peace Conference in 1919 and as Under-Secretary of State during the mid-1920's. (In this latter position he was involved in the implementation of the Rogers Act, which helped to professionalize the U.S. diplomatic service.) He was appointed ambassador to Japan by President Hoover in 1932, arriving in Tokyo in June of that year, and was retained in the post by President Franklin Roosevelt, when he took office the following year.

Although arriving to a situation still tense as a result of the "Manchurian Incident"-- and in the midst of wet, drizzly weather characteristic of Japan's climate during the June rainy season-- Grew nevertheless began his new assignment in high spirits, referring to it in the days just prior to his arrival as a "new adventure in this kaleidoscopic life of ours," and beginning the entry in his diary detailing his first day in the country with the statement, "By golly, what a day!"[2] While he harbored few illusions concerning the work at hand, recognizing both Japan's entrenched interests in Manchuria as well as the possibilities of future acts of aggression and even war, he also stated in his diary his intention to do his "utmost to keep a detached and balanced point of view."[3]

America's policy regarding Japan at the time of Grew's arrival was largely the work of then-Secretary of State Henry Stimson. In response to Japan's action in Manchuria, Stimson, in January of 1932, had sent a note to the Japanese government declaring the U.S. government's unwillingness to recognize the Japanese occupation, finding it to be a violation of the 1928 Kellogg-Briand Pact (which Japan had signed) as

---

[2]Joseph C. Grew, *Ten Years in Japan* (New York: Simon and Schuster, 1944), pp. 7, 3, 6. This work, consisting of Grew's personal diaries and notes covering the entire period of his tenure in Japan, provides a vivid, day-by-day account of his actions and experiences. A later work, *Turbulent Era; A Diplomatic Record of Forty Years, 1904-1945*, published in 1952, includes additional material from Grew's Japan years. I have limited myself to the former source in writing this chapter.

[3]*Ibid.*, p. 3.

well as the United States' earlier Open Door Policy in China.[4] Subsequently known as the "Nonrecognition Policy," or "Stimson Doctrine," this position was later supported by the Assembly of the League of Nations and, along with the Lytton Commission Report which likewise condemned Japanese aggression, led to Japan's formal withdrawal from the League in March of 1933. Stimson's policy, much reviled in Japan, in fact set the tone for U.S. policy for the remainder of the decade, and although Stimson was replaced as Secretary of State by Cordell Hull in the Roosevelt cabinet in 1933, he returned to the cabinet as Secretary of War from 1940 to 1945, and thus continued to play a key role in formulating the government's Japan policy during that period as well.

Largely in agreement with the underlying philosophy of the "Stimson Doctrine" (he later referred to Stimson as "a great and sincere idealist"[5]), Grew nevertheless was also aware of the instability of the internal political situation in Japan at this time. (The "5-15 Incident," an unsuccessful coup attempt by the "younger officer" element in the Japanese army, had taken place while he was crossing the U.S. on his way to assuming his post.) For this reason, in a confidential letter to the Secretary in December of 1932, following the Japanese establishment of the puppet state of Manchukuo in September and the release of the Lytton report shortly thereafter, he counseled "restraint," adding that "[a]ny hint of force, either military or economic, I believe, would result in the uniting of the nation behind the military and would completely overwhelm the more moderate influences which are working beneath the surface to restore Japan to its former high place in the councils of nations."[6]

In the years ahead Grew stuck to this position as events moved closer to the point of ultimate conflict. A firm believer in the need to focus on the "facts, conditions, and circumstances" of a particular diplomatic situation rather than to apply hard and fast "theories" (a carefully couched criticism perhaps of the idealism of Stimson),[7] it was

---

[4]The Kellogg-Briand Pact pledged the signatories to the renunciation of war as an instrument of foreign policy; the Open Door Policy dated from a turn of the century statement by the U.S. regarding the preservation of the territorial integrity of China and the right of all countries to pursue trade there on a free and equal basis.

[5]Grew, p. 88.

[6]*Ibid.*, p.70.

[7]Grew outlined his general thoughts on this subject in a diary entry entitled "Can Any Peace Pact Keep the Peace" (February 23, 1933), *Ibid.*, pp.78-80. (The quoted items are from p. 80.)

nevertheless no naive appeasement or overly-optimistic hope that he indulged in. At one point, in December of 1934, he criticized in his diary an American senator's advocacy of legislation to appease Japan, writing that "...he probably does not realize what harm that sort of public statement does in strengthening the Japanese stand and in reinforcing the aggressive ambitions of the expansionists," and in early February of 1936 he gave conditional support to another senator's "inflammatory speech" against Japanese aggression by stating that "I can't help feeling that just once in a while it is healthy to let the Japanese know that fire still exists in what they may believe to be an extinct volcano."[8]

As events moved from the "Three Years of Calm Before the Storm"-- as he was later to refer to the February 1933 to February 1936 period in the published version of his diaries-- to a more critical phase beginning with the second unsuccessful coup attempt by the "younger officer" element (in February of 1936), Grew's level of concern and pessimistic assessment of the situation increased. At the beginning of 1937 he wrote of the parallels existing between the political situation in Japan and that of Germany in the period prior to World World I[?]-- and the year ahead, of course, continued the downward slope. In July the "China Incident," begun like the earlier incident in Manchuria by military action in the field without the approval or foreknowledge of the Tokyo government, marked the onset of the China War, and another significant downturn in U.S.-Japanese relations.

As conditions worsened, Grew continued his efforts to mediate differences rather than issue ultimatums. In these final, critical years prior to the conflict, Grew's involvement in two controversial areas deserves particular mention. The first of these has to do with his role in the decision to impose economic embargoes on Japan.

By the fall of 1937 the question of embargoes on vitally-needed scrap iron and oil shipments to Japan was rapidly becoming a major issue of debate in the U.S. The idea was strongly supported by former Secretary of State Stimson and a number of special interest groups, and Roosevelt himself seemed to be leaning in this direction in a speech delivered in Chicago on October 5th in which he made reference to the need for a "quarantine" of nations involved in aggression.[10] Grew

---

[8]*Ibid.*, pp. 147; 164, 165.

[9]*Ibid.*, p. 192.

[10]Herbert Feis, *The Road to Pearl Harbor; The Coming of the War Between The United States and Japan* (Princeton, N.J.: Princeton University Press, 1971), pp. 11-12.

continued to be opposed to such action, believing that it would almost certainly push Japan into further acts of aggression rather than causing her to pull back from ground already taken.[11]

No specific action was taken on the embargo issue at that time, but in the summer of 1939, just prior to the outbreak of war in Europe, Roosevelt took steps to notify Japan of the formal termination, in six months, of the 1911 commercial treaty still in effect between the two countries, thus paving the way for the possiblity of embargoes in the future.[12] Once again Grew urged against such action,[13] but by September of 1940-- apparently out of frustration resulting from meetings with Japanese Foreign Minister Matsuoka[14]-- he briefly changed his mind, sending what is usually referred to as his "green light" telegram (of September 12, 1940) in which he recommended "a show of force, together with a determination to employ it if need be" in response to Japanese intransigence.[15] The extent to which this telegram influenced subsequent events is a matter of conjecture. It was clearly the movement of Japanese troops into northern Indochina on September 23rd and Japan's projected signing of the Tripartite Treaty with Germany and Italy which were the most immediate causes of the embargo (formally announced on September 26, 1940),[16] but there is little question that Grew's telegram played a part in the process. By the end of the month Grew had reversed himself on the question, returning once again to his original position of the inadvisability of such action if war was to be averted, but the corner had definitely been turned.[17]

---

[11]See Grew, p. 80; p. 221 for a specific reference to the likely failure of sanctions in the aftermath of Roosevelt's speech.

[12]George Brown Tindall, *America; A Narrative History*, 2nd ed., Vol. 2 (New York: Norton, 1988), p. 1169.

[13]Feis, p. 41; Grew, p. 305.

[14]Matsuoka Yosuke (1880-1946) was an outspoken proponent of Japan's expansionist policies. As Japan's chief delegate to the League of Nations, he led Japan out of that body in 1933, and as foreign minister in the second Konoe cabinet (July 22, 1940-July 18, 1941) he concluded the Tripartite Treaty with Germany and Italy. Following the war he was indicted as a class-A war criminal but died before his trial was completed. At first Grew seems to have harbored some hope of dealing with this individual (see Grew, pp. 328-9), but this quickly gave way to frustration (see pp. 330ff.)

[15]Feis, pp. 101-2.

[16]*Ibid*.., p. 106.

[17] On October 1 he hints once again at the likely Japanese response to sanctions, particularly in providing "telling reasons for those groups in Japan which desire to obtain political and economic security by acquiring

Although some commentators find his subsequent advice ambiguous,[18] Grew seems to have maintained his basic opposition to embargoes and other types of economic sanctions down through the crisis of July 1941 (which saw the freezing of Japanese funds in the U.S. and the embargo extended to oil in the aftermath of the Japanese move into southern Indochina), and into the late summer and early fall of that year as well.[19] By that time, of course, he was deeply embroiled in a second major area of controversy connected with the diplomacy of the period, the proposed meeting between Japanese Prime Minister Konoe and President Roosevelt as a last ditch effort to resolve the differences between the two countries.

The idea of a face-to-face meeting between the two leaders first surfaced in early August of 1941. Konoe, never the most forceful or consistent of political leaders,[20] seemed genuinely troubled by the preceding month's events and the critical stage they signaled in U.S.-Japanese relations. While holding mixed views on the Japanese leader,[21]

---

sources of raw materials and markets entirely under Japanese domination" (Grew, p. 336).

[18]See Feis, pp. 137 (n.7); 271.

[19]While his diary entries and notes provide no specific criticism of the U.S. action taken in July, he makes note in a report to Washington dated September 29, 1941 of the need for making a choice between "the method of progressive economic strangulation or the method of constructive concilliation," stating that to his mind the latter course should be "the definite choice of the United States Government" (Grew, p. 438).

[20]A descendant of the Fujiwara family of ancient Japan (and grandfather of the recent (1993-4) Japanese prime minister, Hosokawa Morihiro), Konoe Fumimaro (1891-1945) served as prime minister of Japan from June 4, 1937 to Jan. 5, 1939 and again between July 22, 1940 and Oct. 18, 1941. He was thus in office at the time of such crucial events as the "China Incident" and the beginning of the war with China in July of 1937, the announcement of the "New Order in Asia" (Nov. 1938) and its successor the "Greater East Asia Co-prosperity Sphere" (Aug. 1940), and the finalizing of the Tripartite Treaty with Germany and Italy (Sept. 1940). Described as "polished and urbane" (Gordon M. Berger, "Conflict, Compromise, and Tragedy: Konoe Fumimaro and Tojo Hideki" in *Great Historical Figures of Japan* (Tokyo: Japan Culture Institute, 1978), p. 297) but also "weak and vacillating" (*Kodansha Encyclopedia of Japan* (Tokyo: Kodansha, 1983), vol. 4, p. 273), he committed suicide in December of 1945 on the day he was to be arrested for trial as a war criminal by the Occupation authorities.

[21]See for example negative assessments (Grew, pp. 324, 329, 354) countered by more positive, even glowing, appraisals (pp. 420, 481-2), probably reflecting once again the inconsistent character of the man.

Grew strongly supported the idea of the meeting as the last real chance
for avoiding conflict. In a telegram to Secretary of State Hull dated
August 18th he urged "that this Japanese proposal not be turned aside
without very prayerful consideration."[22] Hull, however, did not favor
such a meeting. A firm believer in the application of fixed principles to
questions of international affairs-- he later wrote in his memoirs of his
belief in the existence of "solid, living, all-essential rules" which if
followed by the world would lead to peace but which if not followed
would lead to an "eternal" state of war-- he did not believe that the
Japanese government, given its past record, was doing anything other
than simply searching for a way to buy time in which to consolidate its
territorial gains.[23] Despite Grew's repeated warnings over the course of
the next two months that a failure to follow up on the meeting would
lead to the fall of the Konoe government and the passing of the last real
hope for peace, the meeting never took place. In October the Konoe
government fell, replaced by that of the militarist, General Tojo, and
events continued their downward course toward disaster.

Holding out little hope of avoiding conflict, Grew nevertheless
remained in Japan during the critical weeks preceding the Pearl Harbor
attack, doing his best to keep his government apprised of the rapidly
worsening situation there. In a report dated November 3, 1941, he
warned of "Japan's capacity to rush headlong into a suicidal struggle
with the United States," adding that "[w]hile national sanity dictates
against such action, Japanese sanity cannot be measured by American
standards of logic." The report concludes with the ominous statement
that-- "Action by Japan which might render unavoidable an armed
conflict with the United States may come with dangerous suddenness."[24]

Following the December 7th attack and the formal declaration of
war by the U.S. the next day, Grew and his wife remained confined in
the U.S. Embassy compound in Tokyo until a formal exchange of
diplomats between the two countries, worked out by representatives of
the Swiss government, had been implemented. These negotiations were
finally successful and they departed for the U.S. in June of 1942. Upon
his return he served as Under Secretary of State during the later phases
of the war. In this capacity he was the originator of a plan to offer
assurances to the Japanese that they would be allowed to retain the
Emperor system as a means of gaining their surrender in the months

[22]Feis. p. 258.
[23]*Ibid.* , p. 259; the quotation from Hull's *Memoirs* is from the same source,
p. 10.
[24]Grew, pp. 469, 470.

prior to the use of the atomic bomb on Hiroshima and Nagasaki. Unfortunately, the plan did not gain acceptance among top policy-makers in Washington, and the decision to use the bomb went forward.[25] (The idea later, of course, became a crucial part of the final Japanese surrender policy.)

Grew's role in the pre-war and wartime period will long be a subject of debate. By his own account, in the critical period leading up to the war, he was deeply immersed in the particular conditions of his assignment and did not possess the broader view of events held by his superiors in Washington.[26] At the same time, as his experience in his assignment broadened, he was clearly far better informed on those "particulars" than were those back home. Would closer attention to his statements on the effects of economic sanctions have led to a less rigid approach and a different outcome? Would the proposed meeting between Prime Minister Konoe and President Roosevelt in the fall of 1941, which Grew strongly supported, have functioned in any real sense to resolve differences and avert the catastrophe? Could the Japanese surrender later on have been accomplished without recourse to atomic weapons? The answers to such questions, of course, remain ultimately hidden beneath the grim realities of what *actually* took place-- "academic questions" they are sometimes called because of the preceived pointlessness of debating them after the fact-- but if similar cataclysms are to be avoided in the future such questions clearly need to be addressed. The struggle of Joseph Grew against the tides of history thus continues to be a topic of considerable interest and debate.

---

[25]The plan is discussed in Hyoe Murakami, *Japan: The Years of Trial, 1919-52* (Tokyo: Kodansha, 1983), pp. 176-8.
[26]See statements to this effect (Grew, pp. 445, 469).

STUDY/DISCUSSION QUESTIONS FOR
JOSEPH GREW

1. In what sense can the entire history of U.S.-Japan relations from Perry's arrival in Japan in 1853 to December of 1941 be seen, in hindsight, to constitute an 'inexorable flow' toward war? What were some of the 'parallels in development' existing between the two countries during this period? What had been some of their major points of conflict in the past?

2. What were the key events immediately preceeding Joseph Grew's arrival in Japan which served to accelerate the drift toward war? How would you explain these events from the Japanese perspective? How did they look to American policy makers? *Manchurian incident*

3. What were the key developments *following* Grew's arrival which contributed to this process? What steps did Grew take to deal with these issues? How would you describe Grew's overall view of Japan during this period?

4. What was Grew's position regarding economic embargoes? Do you think he was right or wrong on this issue?

5. To what extent do you think the idea of a meeting between President Roosevelt and Japanese Prime Minister Konoe in the late summer of 1941 would have served to avoid war? Was it a mistake not to have followed up on this opportunity?

6. To what extent do you think the 'broader view' of key policy-makers like Secretary of State Hull or Secretary of War Stimson was a more accurate one than Grew's view of the on-the-scene 'particulars'?

7. In the final analysis, was war between the U.S. and Japan avoidable?

8. From what you have read elsewhere, do you think the use of the atomic bomb was necessary to end the war with Japan? Do you think Grew's idea of a promise to the Japanese that they would be allowed to retain their emperor would have led to a quicker Japanese surrender?

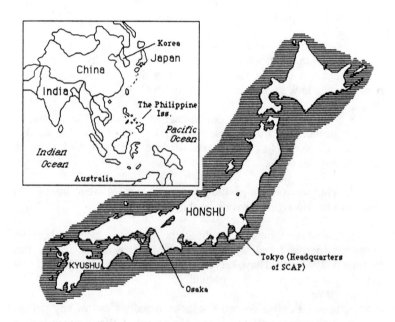

Korea

Japan

China

India

The Philippine
Iss.

Pacific
Ocean

Indian
Ocean

Australia

HONSHU

KYUSHU

Tokyo (Headquarters
of SCAP)

Osaka

Chapter 12

General Douglas MacArthur (1880-1964)

The Postwar Occupation

In sharp contrast to that of Joseph Grew, Douglas MacArthur's relationship with Japan combined the dual roles of wartime adversary and head of the postwar occupation.

Born in Little Rock, Arkansas in 1880, MacArthur followed his father, Gen. Arthur MacArthur, into a military career, graduating from West Point Military Academy at the head of his class in 1903. His first years of service saw him stationed in the Philippines, where his father had served before him, as well as in other parts of East Asia[1] prior to participating in the U.S. occupation of Vera Cruz in 1914 and holding several important commands in Europe in the period during and immediately following the First World War (1917-1919). After the war he served as superintendent of West Point from 1919 to 1922, spent five more years in the Philippines, and from 1930 to 1935 served as Army Chief of Staff at which point he was promoted to the rank of general. The second half of the 1930's saw him returning once again to the Philippines where he served first as a military and later as a civilian

---

[1]His first visit to Japan occurred in 1905 when he served briefly as an aide to his father during an official tour of Asia which the latter made at that time.

advisor (following his initial retirement from the army in 1937) to the
Philippine defense force. It was while serving in this latter capacity, as
relations between the U.S. and Japan rapidly headed toward open
conflict, that he was recalled to active duty by President Franklin
Roosevelt in July of 1941 and placed in command of American troops
in the Far East.

When the Japanese launched their surprise attack on Pearl Harbor
in December of that year MacArthur faced a similar situation in the
Philippines. Within a matter of hours after the Pearl Harbor attack
Japanese airplanes attacked and destroyed over half of the American
planes at Clarke Field near Manilla. The loss of such a significant
number of aircraft eventually led to the American retreat from the
Philippines the following March. Although MacArthur, who had been
predicting that war would not come before April, bore some criticism
for lack of preparedness and failure to respond to the initial attack, his
subsequent retreat to Australia and dramatic parting statement "I shall
return" became a rallying point for American efforts to turn back the
Japanese in the Pacific. Remaining in control of American forces in the
region, MacArthur played a key role in determining the American
strategy, known as "island-hopping," which ultimately led to the defeat
of Japan, and he personally directed the Leyte invasion in October of
1944 which led to the recapture of the Philippines in the later stages of
the war. He was promoted to the rank of five-star general in December
of 1944, and officially presided over the signing of the official Japanese
surrender aboard the U.S. battleship *Missouri* on September 2, 1945.
At this time he had already been appointed to the position of Supreme
Commander for the Allied Powers by President Truman, and it was in
this position that he was to have his most significant and lasting
impact on Japan.

The Supreme Commander for the Allied Powers, or "SCAP" as
the associated administrative body was known, bore ultimate
responsibility for the Allied Occupation of Japan which lasted from
August of 1945 to April of 1952. Although technically a joint venture
undertaken by the eleven nations which had won the war and under the
supervision of an Allied Council comprised of representatives of the
U.S., Great Britain, the Soviet Union and China, SCAP was primarily
a U.S. undertaking, and, in the initial stages at least, it was MacArthur
who served as its principal symbol. Believing that he possessed a true
understanding of the "Oriental Mind," he half consciously and half by
natural inclination cultivated an aloof and imperious style with the
Japanese which they seem to have respected, viewing him as a kind of
shogun, or military dictator, in line with the type of leader characteristic

of earlier periods in Japanese history. (The picture associated with MacArthur's initial arrival in the country to assume his post, in August of 1945, provides a good indication of this style. After the plane carrying him had come to a full stop and the exit ramp had been wheeled into place, a military band broke into a brisk march, at which point, in the words of one biographer: "MacArthur took two steps down [the ramp], puffed twice on his corncob [pipe], and then paused in a dramatic pose for the cameramen, the pipe and his cap set at jaunty angles." An often-published picture taken with the Japanese emperor, Hirohito, in which MacArthur stands with his uniform shirt open at the collar in an informal pose, next to the formally-dressed and much smaller Japanese leader, creates a similiar effect.[2])

The principal goals of the Occupation administration which MacArthur oversaw can be summed up under four general headings: dismemberment (of Japan's colonial empire), demilitarization, punishment, and democratic reform. The first stage involved the dismantling of Japan's enormous colonial empire, which at the war's end was manned and administrated by over three million troops and a nearly equal number of civilians scattered throughout the Asian field of operations. All of these individuals were eventually brought back to Japan, and all troops on the home front were returned to civilian life. To further complete the process of pacification, trials were begun in Tokyo in 1946 to punish military and political leaders judged guilty of war crimes. These proceedings, which lasted until 1948, saw the trials of over 6,000 individuals, including 25 "Class A" or major war criminals such as the wartime prime minister, Tojo. A majority of the individuals tried received prison sentences, and somewhat over nine hundred (Tojo included) were sentenced to death and subsequently executed.[3] In addition, approximately 200,000 former military officers,

[2]Quotation from William Manchester, *American Caesar; Douglas MacArthur, 1880-1964* (Boston: Little, Brown, 1978), p. 445; the photograph with the Emperor can be found, among other places, in Conrad Schirokauer, *A Brief History of Japanese Civilization* (Fort Worth, TX: Harcourt Brace Jovanovich, 1993), p. 267. The earlier reference to MacArthur's self-proclaimed knowledge of the "Oriental Mind" is from the *Kodansha Encyclopedia of Japan* (Tokyo: Kodansha, 1983), vol. 5, p. 78.
[3]Some of the legal aspects of the "Tokyo Trials," including MacArthur's role in overseeing them, have been called into question by later historians (see Richard Minear, *Victors' Justice; The Tokyo War Crimes Trial* (Tokyo: Tuttle, 1972), especially pp. 160-9). A related area of controversy concerns the responsibility of Hirohito, the wartime emperor, some arguing that he too should have been placed on trial as a war criminal (see

business leaders and public officials from the wartime period were officially "purged" (prohibited from holding positions of influence) in the postwar period.[4] Reparations to Southeast Asian countries which had been the victims of Japanese aggression were also assessed, initially in the form of shipments of Japanese industrial equipment, but ultimately as direct cash payments.

In a more positive vein, the Occupation sought to reform the Japanese political, economic and social structure in order to engender the growth of democracy, which Occupation officials including MacArthur believed had existed in only the most rudimentary form previously.[5] Among the specific reforms enacted were: the breaking up of the large, family-owned industrial and financial conglomerates (*zaibatsu*) which Occupation authorities believed had played a key role in supporting wartime aggression; a program of land reform which sought to eliminate absentee land ownership and to make land available at low prices to former tenants; laws to promote the activities of unions and to improve the lot of industrial workers; and a number of attempts at decentralization and reform in such areas as education, police and local government. In addition, a new national constitution, formulated largely by Occupation authorities-- it was originally written in English and *translated* into Japanese-- was promulgated in 1947. This new constitution redefined the role of the emperor (making him merely a symbol of national unity rather than a god), created a more fully democratic Diet (or parliament) with the prime minister and his cabinet fully reponsible to it, gave women the right to vote, and contained an article (Article 9) which renounced war and forbid the establishment of military forces.

MacArthur's precise role in the institution of these reforms remains a matter of debate. Many, of course, were a direct result of his leadership, while others were the work of a variety of individuals of a

---

David Bergamini, *Japan's Imperial Conspiracy: How Emperor Hirohito Led Japan into War Against the West* (New York: Morrow, 1971). MacArthur, wisely one suspects, favored the idea of allowing the Japanese to retain the emperor as a figurehead and as a source of support for Occupation reforms.

[4]Many of those purged later returned to positions of power when the Occupation ended in 1952 (see discussion below).

[5]Actually, a more enlightened reading of Japanese history prior to the 1930's shows a considerable development of democracy, especially during the 1920's. For current material on this subject see essays in Sections VII and XI of Harry Wray and Hilary Conroy, eds., *Japan Examined; Perspectives on Modern Japanese History* (Honolulu: University of Hawaii Press, 1983).

decidedly more liberal bent-- "New Dealers" from the Roosevelt era and "Fair Dealers" from the Truman administration-- for whom MacArthur, with his strong conservative constituency at home, served, unintentionally, as a kind of legitimizing force. Along with their perception of the need for reform, MacArthur and his assistants quickly tuned in as well to the desperate need for economic recovery in the war-devastated nation. Major cities, such as Tokyo and Osaka, lay in ruins, with over half of their houses destroyed by wartime air attacks. There were severe food and fuel shortages. Mass starvation was a real possibility without some form of large-scale relief effort. MacArthur and his forces moved quickly to supply these needs, and as time passed (and especially as the U.S. entered the early years of the Cold War and Japan assumed a new strategic importance in the region) the strengthening of the country's economy took on an even greater significance. By 1947 a "reverse course," which emphasized economic recovery and, ultimately, at least some modified rearmament (in the form of what was later to be called a Self-Defense Force), was rapidly replacing the earlier Occupation themes of punishment and reform. Some liberal political reforms (such as efforts at unionization) were halted. Communists were purged from the government with the support and encouragement of Occupation authorities in the early 1950's, and individuals earlier purged because of their wartime political connections were allowed to move back into positions of prominence. (Hatoyama Ichiro (1883-1959), who became the Japanese prime minister in 1954 after earlier having been purged by Occupation authorities, stands as a prime example of this process.) Before this new direction had fully asserted itself, however, MacArthur's future, as well as that of Japan itself, was greatly effected by an occurrence in a neighboring country--the outbreak of war in Korea.

When North Korean forces, under Communist control, crossed the 38th parallel in June of 1950 and attacked the south,[6] MacArthur was selected as the commander of the United Nations forces sent to defend South Korea. He launched an amphibious attack at Inchon in September of 1950, pushing the North Korean forces back into their own territory, but in November the Chinese entered the battle in support of North Korea, and in April of 1951, in a dispute over the subsequent conduct of the war with President Truman, who accused him of insubordination, MacArthur was relieved of his command. Although he returned to the

---

[6]Korea had been partitioned at the 38th parallel since the end of World War II, North Korea initially under the control of the Soviets and South Korea under the control of the U.S.

U.S. to a hero's welcome and widespread popular support it was his last moment in the limelight. After the initial controversy surrounding his dismissal died down he lived out the remainder of his life in quiet retirement in New York city, finally dying in 1964 at the age of eighty-four.

Just as the Korean War proved to be the end of MacArthur's career, it had a profound effect, albeit it in a much more positive manner, on Japan's future as well. With the onset of the war the strategic importance of Japan took on an even greater import, and its proximity to the field of action brought lucrative orders for equipment and supplies which played a key role in the revitalization of the Japanese economy. In April of 1952 the Occupation which MacArthur had earlier directed came to an end with the signing of a formal peace treaty.

Historians continue to debate both the long-term effects of the Allied Occupation as well as MacArthur's role in it. Did the Occupation, as some claimed at the time, mark a complete reversal in Japanese affairs and constitute "one of the most fascinating and important chapters in the history of the world in modern times," or did it merely continue a pattern of development (in the direction of democracy and economic growth) which had already been underway in pre-war Japan?[7] To what degree did MacArthur himself contribute the key ideas-- the land reform program, the "reverse course" of the post-1947 period-- which were to have such a lasting impact on Japan's future?[8]

However one answers these questions, the larger character of the Occupation itself as an extraordinary and largely unprecedented endeavor, and MacArthur's place as the preeminent symbol of it, can scarcely be denied.

---

[7]See once again the series of essays in Section XI of Wray and Conroy, *Japan Examined, op. cit.* The quotation, by historian Edwin Reischauer, is from p. 332 of that work.

[8]Michael Schaller in *Douglas MacArthur; The Far Eastern General* (New York: Oxford University Press, 1989) provides interesting insights on this question, noting especially how personal political ambitions sometimes played a role in MacArthur's decision-making (see especially chapters 9 and 10).

STUDY/DISCUSSION QUESTIONS FOR
GENERAL DOUGLAS MACARTHUR

1. Describe briefly the key events of MacArthur's relationship with Japan in the years before and during the Pacific War. How would you describe the overall character of that relationship?

2. In what ways was MacArthur an ideal choice to head the postwar Occupation? Be sure to consider personal characteristics, as well as such larger issues as earlier career, political background, etc.

3. What were the original goals of the Occupation? What were the particular actions, programs, etc. undertaken to achieve these goals?

4. How did the original goals of the Occupation change over time? What was the role of the Cold War in bringing about these changes? In what other ways did the Cold War effect Japan?

5. How did the Cold War effect MacArthur's career?

6. What do you feel were the most lasting contributions of the Occupation to subsequent Japanese development?

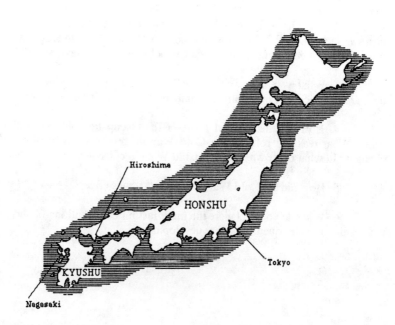

Chapter 13

Ruth Benedict
(1887-1948)

An Academic's Wartime Service:
The Writing of *The Chrysanthemum and the Sword*

Despite the animosities unleashed by the Pacific War, not all wartime activities in the U.S. led to an increased hatred for and a propagandistic, stereotypical view of the enemy. One of the most extraordinary works to come out of the wartime period (and one with important long-term implications for policy-makers) was a study written by a woman who, like Arthur Waley earlier, never set foot in Japan. The work was *The Chrysanthemum and the Sword*, and the author, the world famous anthropologist, Ruth Benedict. Benedict came to the writing of her classic study of the Japanese as the result of an attempt to place her academic background and training in the wartime service of her country. In this manner it provides an interesting case study in the interplay of wartime patriotism and academic impartiality.

Ruth Benedict (maiden name Ruth Fulton) was born in 1887 in upper New York state. She attended Vassar College in the early years of the century (1905-1909), majoring in English literature, and after experimenting briefly with careers in teaching and social work, married Stanley Benedict, a biochemist, in 1914. During the early years of what

proved to be a childless and unhappy marriage, she continued to cast
about for a source of direction in her life, finally discovering the field of
anthropology through a series of lectures which she attended in 1919 at
the New School for Social Research in New York City. In 1921 she
entered Columbia University where she completed a doctorate under
Franz Boas, one of leading figures in the discipline, and in 1923 she
joined the faculty at Columbia, undertaking, among other activities, the
editorship of the *Journal of American Folklore*, a position which she
held from 1925 to 1939. During this period as well, she did extensive
field research, much of it among Native American tribes of the
Southwest, and published widely in academic journals. In 1934 she
published her seminal work, *Patterns of Culture*, in which she
developed the larger theoretical framework for her ideas concerning the
manner in which culture and individual behavior interact. By 1939 then,
as the Second World War began, she had clearly attained a position of
eminence in her field.[1]

The threat of war weighed heavily on Benedict, as it did upon
many intellectuals. It effected both her mental and emotional outlook as
well as the character and direction of her academic work. "I feel very far
out of the world, but at least I know no world conflagation has flared up
yet" she wrote in August of 1939, just two weeks before the beginning
of the war in Europe.[2] Like many intellectuals, the onset of war, and
the consideration of the values being articulated concerning it, led
Benedict to speak out publicly on the need to overcome race prejudice in
the U.S. and on the closely-related need for maintaining academic
freedom during the wartime period.[3] In a more specific sense she also
sought ways in her own writing and research to bring her particular
academic background to bear on the larger ethical and policy-making

---

[1] Biographical information summarized from Margaret Mead, *Ruth Benedict*
(N.Y.: Columbia Univ. Pr., 1974) and from the same author's entry in the
International Encyclopedia of the Social Sciences (N.Y.: Crowell Collier &
Macmillan, 1968), vol. 2, pp. 48-52.
[2] Quoted in Margaret M. Caffrey, *Ruth Benedict: Stranger in This Land*
(Austin, TX: Univ. of Texas Pr., 1989), p. 292.
[3] Both directions are discussed in Caffrey, pp. 302-3. Benedict's decision
during this period to write a popular book on the science of race (published
under the title *Race: Science and Politics* in 1940) provides further evidence
of her willingness to dedicate time and energy to combating racial
intolerance.

considerations of the day. One of her efforts in this latter direction was an essay, written in the fall of 1939, which set out to consider the subject of war itself from an anthropological perspective. Entitled "The Natural History of War," the essay defined war as "homicide in a blaze of glory" exercised against members of an external group, as opposed to murder which consisted of "homicide with penalties" exercised against individuals within one's own group. In Benedict's view, war was by no means an absolute in the human condition; some primitive tribes, for example, existed without any concept of war whatsoever. Among groups where war existed-- which of course constituted the majority of the world's cultures-- she went on to distinguish between war conducted in a "socially nonlethal" manner, such as among American Indian tribes where warfare had a kind of symbolic or ritual character and was not directed at conquering or subjugating the enemy, and "sociologically lethal forms of war" which existed where these latter goals were predominant. Although not published until some twenty years later (in 1959), the essay offers clear evidence of Benedict's state of mind at the time of the European war's beginning. While by no means arguing a position of total pacifism, the essay's application of anthropological perspectives to the prevailing international situation raised serious questions regarding the overall value and usefulness of war as a means of dealing with international differences. [4]

In her work which followed, Benedict continued to seek ways of understanding international conflict through the analysis of anthropological data. Why were some cultures, for example, peaceable and benign in regard to their neighbors, while others were inherently aggressive and a constant threat to those around them? [5] At the same time, she also struggled with the conflict existing between the academic's need to maintain objectivity in the study of other cultures and her moral responsibility as a citizen to take a stand regarding

---

[4]The essay appears in Margaret Mead, *An Anthroplogist at Work; Writings of Ruth Benedict* (Boston: Houghton Mifflin, 1959). Quotations used here are from the 1977 Greenwood Press reprint of this work, pp. 371 and 373 respectively.

[5]See discussion in Caffrey, pp. 304-12. Among the conclusions she came to was the importance of what she called "synergy" (defined as a capacity for "combined action") within cultures. Individuals in cultures with high synergy levels, in Benedict's analysis, were happy and contented and thus peace-loving, while those in cultures with low synergy levels were frustrated, fractious and warlike (see pp. 308-9).

unacceptable forms of behavior in the world. In the words of one biographer--

> Her private feeling [in this regard] was that cultures should be left to go their own way, no matter how seemingly pathological, as long as they did not harm other cultures. She could accept Nazi Germany as the zoologist accepted and studied the rattlesnake as a part of the universe. But if a snake hurt others, it had to be defanged or destroyed.[6]

During this time as well she also became involved in her first form of war-related government service-- in the area of diet and national defense. In early 1941 she was invited to become a member of a committee set up under the National Research Council to coordinate government nutrition programs in preparation for possible U.S. entry into the war. She attended monthly meetings of this group in Washington over the course of the next two years, and did local work on its behalf in her home area.

When the Japanese attack on Pearl Harbor occurred in December of 1941 and the U.S. formally entered the war, Benedict continued to speak out on the side of academic balance and restraint. She continued her attack on race discrimination in the U.S., and although she supported the government's program of relocating Japanese-Americans in the early stages of the war she publicly upheld the loyalty of these individuals and stressed the need for preserving their basic civil rights. Like many intellectuals of the period she also became a firm supporter of a postwar "United Nations," writing in October of 1942 that

> If we are to prevent the consummation of Hitler's plans we must have a plan which is equally radical and equally tailored to the world as it has become as a result of modern invention. [There are] two alternatives which could keep the world in order: Hitler's or a United Nations.[7]

Despite the activities noted above, Benedict did not move to a more direct form of government service until mid-1943. At that time a growing awareness of the need for a better understanding of foreign

[6]Caffrey, p. 309.
[7]Quoted in Judith Schachter Modell, *Ruth Benedict; Patterns of a Life* (Philadelphia: Univ. of Pennsylvania Pr., 1983), p. 276.

cultures on the part of wartime policy-makers and her belief in the
contribution which applied anthropology might make in this area led
her to accept a full-time position with the Office of War Information in
Washington. She moved to that city, and began this work in the
summer of 1943. At OWI her job involved the production of cultural
surveys of various countries important to the Allied war effort. Her
work commenced with a study of Rumania, a country at that time
under the control of Germany, and from there she moved to a survey of
Thai culture-- Thailand being a country of considerable importance in
the Pacific theater of the war because of its role as an ally of Japan.
Finally, of course, her work at OWI led her to what was to become her
most significant and important undertaking during this period, her
cultural study of Japan.[8]

    Benedict's work at OWI, and the cultural studies which flowed
from it, need to be seen within the larger context of an effort underway
on several fronts at this time to discover ways of studying foreign
cultures when the presence of war rendered firsthand observation and
field work in the countries in question impossible. In 1941 a group
including fellow anthropologist Margaret Mead and her husband,
Gregory Bateson, founded the Council (later *Institute*) for Intercultural
Relations which began the production of so-called "national character"
studies as a contribution to the war effort. The members of this group
pioneered many of the techniques-- interviews with natives of countries
under study who were living abroad, the use of cultural artifacts,
especially films, to achieve larger cultural insights-- which would later
be used by Benedict in her work. Such investigations eventually came
to be known by the term, "the study of culture at a distance." Benedict,
at first only tangentially involved but later, after assuming the position
at OWI, as a more active member of this group, contributed
significantly to its growing store of techniques and methodologies.[9]

---

[8]Mead, *Ruth Benedict*, p. 57-9; Caffrey, pp. 317-21, 328. (Mead and Caffrey
differ regarding the order of Benedict's early work at OWI, Caffrey stating
that her work on Thai culture preceded the Rumanian study.) Benedict also
produced shorter, more specialized studies on a number of other countries as
part of her work at OWI (see Caffrey, p. 320; Mead, *Ruth Benedict*, p. 59).
[9]Caffrey, pp. 319ff., 328; Mead, *An Anthpologist at Work*, pp. 351-3, 558
(n. 19); Mead, *Ruth Benedict*, 57, 58ff. The latter source in particular (p.
59) mentions her early work in literature as providing another important
skill and source of material for cultural analysis. Caffrey (p. 321) offers a
brief discussion of the cross-fertilization of ideas which ultimately gave
birth to the techniques and methodologies involved in "the study of culture

Benedict began her work on Japan in the early summer of 1944,[10] bringing to it the full range of techniques developed by "the study of culture at a distance" group. She read everything she could find on the subject, including translations of Japanese books (since she did not have sufficient time to master the particularly-difficult Japanese language), viewed films produced in Japan, and established a circle of cultural informants, chiefly Japanese-Americans, from whom to gather information and upon whom to test her ideas and theories as they took shape. The first results of her work were a series of memos on various specialized topics relating to Japan, including one which argued for the retention of the emperor in the postwar period. The long term outcome was the writing of *The Chrysanthemum and the Sword*, which she began just shortly after the war ended.[11]

The Chrysanthemum and the Sword then is a work which both looks back (in terms of its origins) to the wartime period and forward into the postwar years. What are its major conclusions, and in what ways does it reflect both of these directions?

First of all, the book's overriding purpose was to understand a former enemy. The opening sentence of the work reads, "The Japanese were the most alien enemy the United States had ever fought in an all-out struggle." The author goes on to state that the Japanese "did not

---

at a distance," as well as the key role played by Benedict in this process. See also Margaret Mead and Rhoda Metraux, eds., *The Study of Culture at a Distance* (Chicago: Univ. of Chicago Pr., 1953) for a more complete summary of the techniques evolved by those engaged in this work.

[10]Benedict's work followed a number of earlier studies on that subject. Geoffrey Gorer, who Benedict had replaced at OWI, for example, had himself produced two such works. Gorer's investigations, at least parts of which focused on Japanese child-rearing practices, had apparently come under criticism, in the words of one of Benedict's biographers, for being more "psychoanalytical than practical," and for constituting what some in the government saw as a kind of "'egghead' research" (Caffrey, p. 319). Benedict, in her own work, clearly sought to take such earlier studies to a new level, as well as to render her work of more immediate practical value to those in charge of establishing policy. Gorer's works, along with several other wartime studies of Japanese character and culture (see works by Haring, LaBarre, Leighton and Meadow), are listed in the bibliography following Edward Norbeck and George De Vos, "Japan," Chapter 2 of Francis L. K. Hsu's *Psychological Anthropology* (N.Y.: Dorsey, 1961), pp. 42-7.

[11]Caffrey, pp. 321-2.

belong to the Western cultural tradition," and that their culture presented Occidentals with a series of basic "contradictions" which rendered their wartime behavior particularly difficult for those outside of their culture to understand-- they are "both aggressive and unaggressive, ...militaristic and aesthetic, ...insolent and polite, rigid and adaptable, submissive and resentful of being pushed around, loyal and treacherous, [etc.]."[12] The book then moves to a discussion of methodological concerns, but in the next chapter, entitled "The Japanese in the War," Benedict continues the attempt to understand Japanese wartime behavior-- territorial expansion, treatment of prisoners of war, and the willingness to fight in the face of overwhelming odds-- by viewing these topics from a "Japanese" rather than a Western perspective.

Beginning with chapter three, the focus of the work moves to an analysis of the deeper forces at work within Japanese culture. The picture which emerges is that of a people whose patterns of behavior are controlled by a set of rigid, commonly-held beliefs-- in social hierarchy, in a nearly endless series of duties and obligations extending down through society, and in a deeply-inculcated moral code stressing duty and honor above personal fulfillment. The view of the Japanese offered is a highly sympathetic one, and the reader comes away with an understanding of the underlying causes of Japanese behavior which, while difficult to understand fully from a Western viewpoint, nonetheless reflects a great advance over the cultural stereotype of the Japanese as a cruel and heartless enemy presented in most wartime propaganda. A final chapter, entitled "The Japanese Since VJ-Day," continues the essentially positive portrayal of the subject. Japanese pragmatism and the ability to learn from past mistakes with a minimum of time lost in difficult and gut-wrenching transitions, helps account for their rapid postwar regeneration. Summing up this point the author writes that "It has been incredible to American occupying troops that these friendly people are the ones who had [earlier] vowed to fight to the death with bamboo spears."[13] The book then, while clearly growing out of the wartime experience, moves far beyond it in pointing the way toward an entirely new view of the Japanese in the postwar world.

As history shows, the view of Japan in the U.S. altered radically in the years following the war. The cooperative and highly-amicable demeanor of the Japanese people during the early stages of the

[12]Ruth Benedict, *The Chrysanthemum and the Sword; Patterns of Japanese Culture* (Boston: Houghton Mifflin, 1989), pp. 1, 2.
[13]*Ibid.*, pp. 304-5, 306.

Occupation, coupled with the changing balance of power in Asia (the onset of the Cold War with the Soviet Union, the growth of Communism in China), lent a whole new perspective to U.S.-Japanese relations. From wartime enemy, Japan began the move to Cold War ally, and with this came an entirely new view of the Japanese people and their culture. *The Chrysanthemum and the Sword*, published in the fall of 1946, both reflected as well as contributed to this changing view. The book was widely read by policy-makers, and, while by no means achieving bestseller status, it was widely reviewed and commented upon.[14] Although a number of its conclusions have come under attack by later scholars, it continues to be widely-read for the insights it offers into even modern day Japanese culture.[15]

This study then, written by an individual who never set foot on Japanese soil nor even came close to mastering its highly-complex and difficult language, stands as a truly remarkable achievement-- and as the culmination as well of an academic's efforts to bring the techniques and insights of her academic work into the wartime service of her country.

[AUTHOR'S NOTE: Benedict's observations concerning the role of women in Japan]

In *The Chrysanthemum and the Sword*, Benedict, in addition to her general analysis of Japanese culture, offers a number of interesting observations on the traditional role of women in Japan.

Clearly women occupied a lower level of status than men in traditional Japanese culture. Even as educational opportunities became available to them as a result of Meiji (late 19th century) reforms, this second-class status continued. (Benedict cites the example of one educational authority of that era who supported the study of foreign languages by upper middle class women so that they would be "able to put their husband's books in the bookcase right side up after they had dusted them.") While Japanese women, overall, tended to fare better

---

[14]Caffrey, pp. 325-6, and Sheila K. Johnson, *The Japanese Through American Eyes* (Stanford, CA: Stanford Univ. Pr., 1988), pp. 14-15, both provide useful information regarding its publishing history.

[15]For a critique of Benedict's work, as well as that of several others involved in doing wartime character studies of the Japanese, see Richard H. Minear, "The Wartime Studies of Japanese National Character" in *The Japan Interpreter*, Vol. 13, No. 1 (Summer 1980), pp. 36-59.

than their counterparts in other Asian countries-- no tradition of footbinding, for example, existed among the upper classes such as existed in China-- Japanese women generally exercised their power from behind the scenes. They maintained almost complete control over their family's finances [a phenomenon which continues to exist to a large extent today], and the dominance of the Japanese mother-in-law (who exercised complete control over her son's wife in the traditional Japanese family) was proverbial. In this latter regard, wives, generally, existed at the outer edges of their husband's "circles of obligations," with it being considered bad form for a husband to show a greater degree of concern or affection for his wife than, say, for his parents or his country.

Since child-bearing existed as the principle source of status for a woman, an unmarried or childless woman (or a woman unable to produce a son) was traditionally looked down upon. Since male children were considered more important than female children, Japanese mothers clearly deferred to the wishes of their sons, often putting up with insufferable behavior (tantrums, even physical pommelings) because of their higher status [and the knowledge, one might add, that they would eventually be disciplined into the harsh, male values of the society by the Japanese educational system]. As is true of many cultures, Benedict found that lower class status generally required less circumscribed behavior (and thus brought a greater degree of freedom) for women [although one imagines that this was offset at the same time by the well-known hardships and difficulties of the Japanese peasant lifestyle]. Age also seemed to bring a corresponding relaxation in the rigidity of proscribed behavior for women.

Overall, viewed through the lens of her anthropological training and background, Benedict's discussion of Japanese women makes interesting reading, while displaying at the same time intriguing connections to contemporary patterns of Japanese culture.[16]

---

[16]One thinks, for example, of the role of husbands and wives in contemporary Japan-- where one finds much less emphasis on romance and love and a far greater emphasis on reciprocal duties than one finds in the West-- and of the obvious deference paid to males within the society, while women continue to wield a considerable amount of power behind the scenes. (For material discussed and quoted in this section see references under the heading, "Women," in the index to Benedict's work.)

STUDY/DISCUSSION QUESTIONS FOR
RUTH BENEDICT

1. How did Ruth Benedict's academic training and background prepare her for the writing of *The Chrysanthemum and the Sword?* What obvious handicaps did she face in undertaking this project?

2. Consider the problems faced generally by "the study of culture at a distance" group. What techniques and methodologies did they develop in the attempt to overcome these difficulties?

3. In what ways did Benedict's study look backward to the wartime period? In what ways did it point forward into the postwar era?

4. What general conclusions about the Japanese did Benedict reach in her work?

5. What were Benedict's principle conclusions regarding the role of women in Japan? To what extent are these true today?

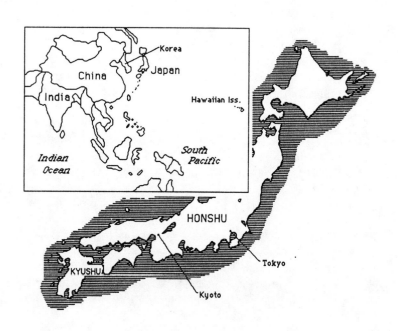

Chapter 14

James Michener
(1907-)

Changing Postwar Attitudes Regarding Japan

Despite its long-term importance, and the role it may have played in setting postwar policy, *The Chrysanthemum and the Sword* did not gain broad, popular readership. The role of overcoming the racial and cultural stereotypes regarding Japan which had grown up during the wartime period belonged to another set of writers who, producing works aimed at a more popular audience in the early part of the 1950's, began the process of recasting the Japanese in a more positive light.[1] One of the first to do this was the bestselling American novelist, James Michener.

Born in New York City in 1907, Michener spent his early years in Pennsylvania, where he attended Swarthmore College. Following his

---

[1] Discussions of wartime propaganda and stereotypes, from the perspective of *both* countries, can be found in such works as John Dower's *War Without Mercy: Race and Power in the Pacific War* (New York: Pantheon Books, 1986) and his more recent collection of essays, *Japan in War and Peace* (New York: New Press, 1993) (especially essays 8 and 9). Sheila K. Johnson's *The Japanese Through American Eyes* (Stanford, CA: Stanford University Press, 1988) (especially chapters 1 and 2) focuses on the American side of the equation.

graduation from there in 1929, he taught in private schools, traveled extensively, and eventually completed a Master's degree in English at the Colorado State College at Greeley (now the University of Northern Colorado) in 1937. He taught briefly there and at Harvard University in the late 1930's and early 1940's, before becoming an associate editor for Macmillan publishing company, assigned to its education division. When World War II broke out, he enlisted in the navy and was stationed in the South Pacific. It was this latter experience which led to his first published work of fiction, *Tales of the South Pacific*, a collection of stories set in that region during the wartime period, which came out in 1947. The book won the Pulitzer Prize for fiction the following year, and was made into a highly-successful Broadway musical, *South Pacific*, by the popular musical comedy team of Rogers and Hammerstein in 1949. Thereafter Michener devoted himself solely to writing, and it was in the early 1950's that Japan became a major topic of interest.

Although the Japanese appear chiefly as wartime adversaries in *Tales of the South Pacific* and its sequel, *Return to Paradise*, published in 1951, it is in his non-fiction work, *The Voice of Asia* (also published in 1951), that the new view of the Japanese begins to assert itself. Based on his recent travels in Japan and other parts of Asia, he begins the section dealing with Japan by referring to the Japanese as "the most cruel and barbarous enemy of modern times," but then goes on to discuss the "miraculous change" which has occurred there since the end of the war. Although attributing this in large part to the postwar Occupation, he also takes note of the fact that "the majority of Americans who served in the Occupation positively liked the country and the people," and he goes on to cite the number of American soldiers who married Japanese women and elected to remain in the country after their term of service ended. (Interestingly, one finds overtones in this work as well of the changing, Cold War perspective of the early 50's and Japan's new role within it, when a former Japanese soldier is quoted as telling the author "that sooner or later [the U.S.] will have to rearm Japan," adding that "we Japanese would never have been kicked around in Korea the way you have been. We know how to fight in such terrain. We understand the Chinese, too. We could do your fighting for you.")[2]

Shortly after the publication of this work Michener produced a widely-read article on Japan for *Holiday* magazine (August 1952),

[2]James A. Michener, *The Voice of Asia* (New York: Random House, 1951), pp. 15-8, 27.

which, according to at least one author,[3] marked the true beginning of the new, postwar view of the country. Focusing largely on traditional arts and culture, he described the beauties and splendors of this culture in places like Tokyo and Kyoto, calling "Japan a land of exquisite beauty [with] a people dedicated to its cultivation."[4] Cold War themes with at least some tangential reference to Japan also appeared in his next work of fiction, *The Bridges at Toko-ri* (serialized in *Life* magazine and published in book form in 1953). Set against the backdrop of the Korean War, the role of Japan as an emerging U.S. ally is highlighted in a scene in that novel where the main character, a U.S. naval pilot named Harry Brubaker, and his family encounter a Japanese family in a hotel bath in Tokyo, and the author writes, "the soft waters of the bath united them. In 1944 Harry had hated the Japanese and had fought gallantly against them, destroying their ships and bombing their troops, but the years had passed, the hatreds dissolved...."[5]

It is in his next work, *Sayonara* (published in book form in 1954), however, that the new, positive view of Japan and the Japanese gets its most popular and extended treatment. Originally serialized in *McCall's* magazine under the title "Sayonara Means Goodbye" in the fall of 1953, *Sayonara* tells the story of Major Lloyd Gruver, a U.S. Air Force officer who comes to Japan after flying combat missions in Korea during the Korean War. Arriving in Japan at the same time is Joe Kelley, a private from his unit, who has gained permission from his superiors to return to Japan to marry a Japanese woman (Katsumi) to whom he had earlier become engaged. Gruver, who soon finds out that his own assignment has been engineered by one of his superiors (General Webster) in order that he might court the General's daughter (Eileen Webster), is initially appalled, as are most of the local military officials, at the prospect of American servicemen marrying Japanese women. Shortly, however, Gruver meets Kelly's bride-to-be and discovers the depth of their feeling for each other. He also witnesses the Japanese woman's utter devotion to her fiance, contrasting it with the aggressive, domineering personality of the General's daughter (and her mother, who he fears she will model herself after), and he begins to question his earlier attitudes. Eventually he falls in love with an actress (Hana-ogi) from a famous Japanese theatrical company and discovers firsthand the attractions of Japanese women. The book focuses

---

[3] See Johnson, *op. cit.*, pp. 94ff.
[4] Quoted in Johnson, p. 94.
[5] James A. Michener, *The Bridges at Toko-ri* (Greenwich, Conn.: Fawcett, 1953), p. 63.

considerable attention upon the cruelty and underlying prejudices of the existing military policy regarding marriages of servicemen to Japanese, a subject upon which the author later published articles in popular magazines.[6] In the end, Joe Kelly and his bride, about to be separated by the military authorities because of a new policy prohibiting such marriages, commit suicide, while Gruver and his Japanese girlfriend also part company, he to pursue his military career (and presumably to marry the General's daughter) and she to remain true to her artistic calling.

The book provides its author with an excellent vehicle, through the experiences of its main character, for the discovery of the "new" Japan. Lloyd Gruver arrives in the country with most of his wartime feelings and prejudices intact: "...I'd been through [Japan] and it had never impressed me much. Dark streets, little paper houses, squat men and fat round women. I had never understood why some Air Force people got so steamed up about Japan." As the novel progresses, however, his views gradually change. At one point he states "...to my surprise I found that I was beginning to enjoy Japanese food," and under the tutelage of Joe Kelly, Hana-ogi and others he gains an understanding of (and appreciation for) such traditional Japanese customs as removing one's shoes before entering a room, sitting on pillows on *tatami* mats, and even the Japanese tradition of ritual suicide.[7] A major focus of this conversion is, of course, his discovery of Japanese women. In comparision to American women, whom he finds cold and domineering-- at one point he compares being in love with Eileen Webster to flying combat missions in Korea[8]-- Japanese women understand the psychological needs of a man and seek only to bring him happiness. (Katsumi, Joe Kelly's bride, for example, uses hot *sake* and a Japanese bath to relax her husband at the end of a hard day, and he tells the Major at one point "...when I see Katsumi I see a dame who

---

[6]See, for example, "Facts About the G.I. Babies," *Reader's Digest* (March 1954), pp. 5-10.

[7]James A. Michener, *Sayonara* (New York: Bantam, 1955), pp. 1, 134, 78, 197-8.

[8]*Ibid.*, p. 54; see also p. 53 for a more direct expression of these feelings ("Mrs. Webster, frankly, had scared the devil out of me and now I could see the same marital tendencies in her daughter. I could see her organizing my life for me solely on the grounds that she loved me, but the definition of what was love would always be *her* definition..."--emphasis added). The book, overall, offers interesting, if largely unconscious, insights into the changing role of women in the U.S. in the 1950's.

could fill my heart for the rest of my life."[9]) This idealization of Japanese women, along with the extended discussion of traditional Japanese culture which the book provides-- one reviewer calls it a virtual "short-order Cook's tour of Japanese art, food, culture, [and] idiom"[10]-- brings the main character (and, one assumes, readers as well) to a much-altered view of the country. Gruver sums up this new attitude when he concludes a lengthy parting soliloquy at the book's end with--

> ...To the alley and the canal and the little houses and the pachinko parlor and to the flutes at night-- sayonara. And you, Japan, you crowded islands, you tragic land-- sayonara, you enemy, you friend.[11]

The new image of Japan presented in *Sayonara* was, of course, further reinforced by the popular Hollywood film based on it. Released in 1957 and starring Marlon Brando as Major Gruver,[12] the cinematic version of the novel contained an even more brimming introduction to Japanese culture, with scenes of *kabuki, noh* and *bunraku* theater, the tea ceremony, *seppuku* (ritual suicide), and numerous examples of Japanese scenery, native costumes and traditional architecture. (It also departed significantly from the book by providing a totally different ending, with Major Gruver saying "sayonara" to both his American fiancee *and* the United States Air Force and about to marry his Japanese girlfriend, Hana-ogi-- and, lest viewers be concerned about the plight of his former fiancee, there is at least the suggestion, toward the end of the film, that *she* is about to enter into a relationship with a Japanese *kabuki* actor, played by the Mexican-born actor, Ricardo Montalban!)

---

[9]*Ibid.*, pp. 95, 13. For a more complete discussion of this view of Japanese women see Johnson, *op.cit.*, chapter 5 ("The Sexual Nexus"), or Karen Ma's treatment of the subject in *The Modern Madame Butterfly; Fantasy and Reality in Japanese Cross-cultural Relationships* (Tokyo: Tuttle, 1995), especially chapter 1 ("Myth of the Modern Madame Butterfly ").

[10]*Time* (January 25, 1954), p. 114.

[11]*Sayonara*, p. 214.

[12]Interestingly, this was not Brando's first excursion into the postwar revitalization of the popular image of things Japanese, since the year before he had played an Okinawan native (!) in the film version of Vern Sneider's 1951 novel, *The Teahouse of the August Moon*, set in Okinawa at the war's end. This novel also played a part in the move to a more positive depiction of Japanese culture in the postwar period, introducing readers, albeit in humorous fashion, to such traditional Japanese arts as the tea ceremony.

Following the publication of *Sayonara*, Michener's interest in Japan remained strong. In the years ahead he published articles dealing with Japan in a number of popular magazines, wrote introductions to several books on the subject, and produced several non-fiction works of his own on Japanese prints, a topic upon which he became a recognized authority.[13] In 1955 he also took as his third wife, Mari Yoriko Sabusawa, an American of Japanese ancestry.

Although he turned to a variety of other subjects in his later work, beginning with the novel *Hawaii* in 1959, his role in creating a more positive image of Japan in the postwar era and in popularizing its traditional culture and customs remains an extremely important one.[14]

[AUTHOR'S NOTE: Japan and the Beat Movement of the 1950's]

Utilizing Japan in an entirely different way and connecting with a totally different audience from the works of James Michener were the writers of the Beat Movement in the U.S. in the 1950's. Comprised of such figures as Allen Ginsberg (1921-), Jack Kerouac (1922-1969), and Gary Snyder (1930-), this group of American writers found in the traditional culture of Japan (as well as a number of other Oriental traditions-- Indian, Chinese, etc.) an alternative to the materialism and conformity of American life in the postwar era-- and their writings served to introduce these subjects as well to the hippy-counterculture generation of the 1960's. Although one can trace the beginnings of this interest in Japan to a number of earlier sources,[15] perhaps no single book did more to popularize these themes, especially among the 1960's generation, than did Jack Kerouac's 1958 novel, *The Dharma Bums*. This work, a thinly-fictionalized account of Kerouac's meeting with Gary Snyder in the period just prior to Snyder's departure for a ten-year

---

[13]For a full listing of these works see the "Selected Bibliography" in A. Grove Day, *James A. Michener* (New York: Twayne, 1964), pp. 157-64.

[14]Even *Hawaii* itself, with the role played by Japanese immigrants in the story and the seminal event of Pearl Harbor in the later portion of the work, displays clear connections to his earlier interests in Japan.

[15]Among them the writings of D.T. Suzuki and Alan Watts on Zen Buddhism, and those of Harold Henderson and R.H. Blyth on Japanese *haiku*. Suzuki, Watts and Henderson all began their publishing careers prior to World War Two, and Blyth's first works date from the late 1940's. Another widely-read author of the early 1950's, J.D. Salinger, utilizes a Zen *koan* as the epigraph to his *Nine Stories*, published in 1953.

(1956-1966) sojourn in Japan,[16] contains references to a number of aspects of Japanese culture, including Zen Buddhism, Japanese gardens, the tea ceremony, Japanese interior design and decor, and *haiku* poetry. Although often containing a superficiality and cultural naivete equaling that of Michener, Kerouac's work views Japanese culture through an entirely different lense (see examples below), and served, along with the works of the other writers noted above, to create yet another, radically different view of Japan in the postwar era.

*   *   *

(Examples of the depiction of Japanese culture in *The Dharma Bums*)

Example #1 - "Japhy Ryder" (Kerouac's fictionalized name for Gary Snyder) introducing "Ray Smith" (Kerouac) to Japanese tea--

... "Did you ever read the Book of Tea?" said he [Ryder].
"No, what's that?"
"It's a scholarly treatise on how to make tea utilizing all the knowledge of two thousand years about tea-brewing. Some of the descriptions of the effect of the first sip of tea, and the second, and the third, are really wild and ecstatic."
"Those guys got high on nothing, hey?"
"Sip your tea and you'll see; this is good green tea." It was good and I immediately felt calm and warm.

Example #2 - "Ray Smith" on Japanese *haiku*--

... Walking in this country you could understand the perfect gems of haikus the Oriental poets had written, never getting

---

[16]Snyder, of all of the "Beats," took the Japanese influence the farthest in his work. A student of Chinese and Japanese languages at the University of California in the mid-1950's, he then studied Zen at Daitoku Temple in Kyoto during his decade-long residence in Japan. His poetry, as early as 1952, showed the influence of Japanese forms (see William J. Higginson, *The Haiku Handbook* (Tokyo: Kodansha, 1989), p. 58), and this influence has continued in his later work as well, which includes studies in the late 1970's of the Ainu cultures of northern Japan.

drunk in the mountains or anything but just going along as
fresh as children writing down what they saw without literary
devices or fanciness of expression. We made up haikus as we
climbed, winding up and up now on the slopes of brush.

Example #3 - "Japhy Ryder" on his forthcoming trip to Japan--

...oh boy I can just see myself in the morning sitting on the
mats with a low table at my side, typing on my portable, and
the hibachi nearby with a pot of hot water on it keeping hot and
all my papers and maps and pipe and flashlight neatly packed
away and outside plum trees and pines with snow on the boughs
and up on Mount Hieizan the snow getting deep and sugi and
hinoki all around, them's redwoods, boy, and cedars. Little
tucked-away temples down the rocky trails, cold mossy ancient
places where frogs croak, and inside small statues and hanging
buttery lamps and gold lotuses and paintings and ancient
incense-soaked smells and lacquer chests with statues.[17]

---

[17]Jack Kerouac, *The Dharma Bums* (N.Y.: Penguin Books, 1976), pp. 19-
20, 59, 205.

STUDY/DISCUSSION QUESTIONS FOR
JAMES MICHENER

1. What would you imagine the depiction of the Japanese to have been like in U.S. popular culture (books, movies, cartoons, etc.) during the wartime period? Have you ever seen any examples of this type of material?

2. What was Michener's original view of the Japanese in his first published fiction-- works such as *Tales of the South Pacific* or *The Return to Paradise*?

3. What do you think were the chief causes of his changing view of Japan in his works published in the early 1950's?

4. In what ways is the changing role of women in the U.S. in the postwar era reflected in Michener's treatment of Japanese women in his novel *Sayonara*?

5. How realistic do you find the altered ending of the movie version of *Sayonara*?

6. How does the work of Michener differ from that of the "Beats" in its use of Japanese culture? Who constituted the respective audiences for these two very different types of literature?

7. How would you describe the current view of Japan in American popular culture? Can you think of any recent examples of this type of material? (See Appendix III-- "Anti-American Sentiments in Recent American Popular Fiction"-- for some examples.)

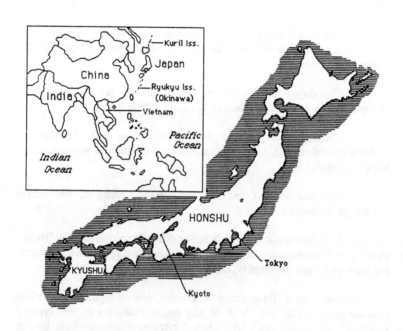

Chapter 15

Edwin O. Reischauer
(1910-1990)

Scholar and Diplomat

It is rare that a professional historian gets the opportunity to turn academic insights into the actual enactment of public policy. One individual who had this opportunity was Edwin O. Reischauer, professor of Japanese history at Harvard University and U.S. Ambassador to Japan from 1961 to 1966.

Edwin Oldfather Reischauer (his middle name came from his mother's maiden name) was born in Tokyo in 1910. His parents were Presbyterian missionaries and teachers, and his father, August Reischauer (1879-1971), was himself the author of several books on comparative religion and missionary work. After graduating from the American School in Tokyo in 1927, Edwin attended Oberlin College in Ohio where he majored in history, graduating Phi Beta Kappa in 1931. He received an M.A. from Harvard University in 1932 and did further study at the University of Paris, Tokyo and Kyoto Universities in Japan, and in Korea and China before receiving his Ph.D. in Far Eastern Languages from Harvard in 1938. He taught at Harvard from 1938 until 1942, when he took a leave of absence to assume a post with the War Department during the early years of World War II. In 1943 he enlisted in the U.S. Army, where he served in military intelligence, helping to break and decipher the Japanese military code. He remained in the army

until the end of the war, attaining the rank of lieutenant colonel and
receiving the Legion of Merit for his work.[1] It was during his last
months in the service, after the war's end, that he produced the
manuscript for what was to be his first book, a short survey of Japanese
history based on a set of lectures he had prepared as part of a training
course for Army intelligence officers during the war. Published in 1946
under the title *Japan Past and Present*, this work has gone through
numerous editions and revisions and, under the new title adopted in
1970, *Japan: The Story of a Nation*, remains in print to the present
day.[2]

　　　Following his discharge from the military, Reischauer worked
briefly for the State Department on a variety of assignments relating to
the Far East and the postwar occupation of Japan, among them the
drafting of policy statements on the future of the emperor system in
Japan, the disposition of captured territories (i.e., the Kuril and Ryukyu
islands), and, unfortunately without success, on planning for the
eventual reunification of Korea. He resigned this post in the fall of
1946 to return to his teaching position at Harvard, where, four years
later, he was promoted to the rank of full professor in the field of
Japanese history.

　　　During the years which followed Reischauer gradually enhanced
his reputation as a scholar and teacher. *East Asia: The Great Tradition*,
co-authored with China specialist John K. Fairbank, was published in
1960 and became a standard textbook for Asian history courses around
the country. He produced numerous other books and scholarly articles,
and often spoke out on policy issues relating to Asia.[3] It was this
growing reputation as an Asian specialist and scholar which gained him
the appointment as U.S. Ambassador to Japan in April of 1961.

---

[1]While Reischauer's background and understanding of Japanese culture
clearly gave him a greater degree of sympathy for the Japanese than many
other policy-makers of the day, an often-told story that he used his position
to spare the historic city of Kyoto from wartime bombing attacks is untrue
(see his statement to this effect in *My Life Between Japan and America* (New
York: Harper & Row, 1986), p. 101).

[2]This first book was dedicated to the memory of his brother, Robert Karl
Reischauer, a promising young academic who, as a civilian, was killed
accidently in Shanghai during the early months of the China War in 1937.

[3]*The United States and Japan*, published in 1950, and *Wanted: An Asian
Policy*, in 1955, were widely read. The former takes a highly optimistic
view of Japan's future in the final stages of the Occupation, while the latter
criticizes America's Cold War foreign policy in Asia.

U.S.-Japan relations in the early 1960's were at something of a
low point. During the decade of the 1950's, under the leadership of the
dominant Liberal Democratic Party (LDP), the country had seen a
gradual pulling back from many of the liberal reforms of the early
Occupation years, and the government had come under increasing attack
from the political left.[4] In 1960, when the Mutual Security Treaty with
the U.S., which authorized the presence of U.S. military bases in Japan
and in effect weddedJapan to U.S. foreign policy, came up for revision
there were widespread demonstrations throughout the country. Despite
the fact that the government of Prime Minister Kishi gained significant
improvements in the terms of the treaty,[5] the unrest led to the
cancellation of a planned visit to Japan by President Eisenhower in June
of that year and the eventual fall of the Kishi government. Reischauer,
in an article in *Foreign Affairs* magazine in October of 1960, had been
sharply critical of the manner in which then-ambassador Douglas
MacArthur II (a nephew of the general) and his staff had handled the
situation, and it was against this backdrop that he was offered the
ambassadorship by President Kennedy when the latter took office the
following year. Despite some misgivings (and the reluctance of his
wife, Haru, who feared a negative response by the Japanese to her
recently-acquired American citizenship[6]) he accepted the post.

The Reischauers arrived in Japan on April 19, 1961, and from the
moment they set foot on Japanese soil the appointment proved to be a
tremendous success. The Japanese, who already knew a great deal about
Reischauer because of his long association with the country, were
particularly pleased to have an ambassador (the first in the history of
U.S.-Japanese relations) who was fluent in Japanese. In addition, his
marriage to a former Japanese citizen, rather than a liability proved a

---

[4]Despite its name, the Liberal Democratic Party (*Jiyu Minshuto*) represents
a relatively conservative position in Japanese politics, counterbalancing
the parties of the left (i.e., the Democratic Socialist (*Minshu Shakaito*),
Socialist (*Nihon Shakaito*), and Communist (*Nihon Kyosanto*) Parties).

[5]Limits were placed on the uses, both inside and outside of Japan, to which
the U.S. forces could be put, and the treaty itself could be terminated after
ten years if either government so desired.

[6]He had married Haru Matsukata, a Japanese journalist, following the death
of his first wife, in 1956. She has related the story of her own life, as well
as that of her interesting and influential forebears, in *Samurai and Silk: A
Japanese and American Heritage* (Cambridge, MA: Harvard University
Press, 1986). Her fears regarding acceptance by the Japanese were
groundless, since both she and her husband were received with enormous
enthusiasm in Japan (see subsequent discussion).

great popular hit. In the years ahead he worked to repair what he had earlier referred to as "the broken dialogue"[7] between the U.S. and Japan. His work paved the way for the crucial decision to return Okinawa to Japan (finalized in 1972) and generally improved the relationship between the two countries. Only one serious personal incident marred his five-year tenure. On March 24, 1964 he was attacked with a knife by a mentally-unbalanced youth while attending an official dinner. The wound he received proved quite serious, requiring several hours of surgery, massive blood transfusions and an extended period of convalescence, and left him with long-term health problems,[8] although he was eventually able to resume his work.

Reischauer remained in his post until 1966. By that time the U.S., under President Johnson, was becoming more and more deeply involved militarily in Vietnam, a direction which Reischauer opposed, calling it a "terrible mistake."[9] In December of 1965, while still at his post, he made a brief tour of U.S. bases in South Vietnam, which generally served to confirm his earlier judgement. Increasingly out of sync with the policies of Johnson and Secretary of State Dean Rusk, and tired after five years on the job, he resigned the ambassadorship in August of 1966.

Returning to Harvard, Reischauer remained in academic life until his retirement in 1981. During this time he continued his contacts with Japan, making numerous trips there in the years both before and after his retirement. His last major work on Japan, *The Japanese*, was published in 1977 and was widely read. He died on September 1, 1990. Although his writings have been to some extent superseded by the work of a younger generation of historians, many of whom he helped to train, the place of Edwin Reischauer in both the academic study of Japan and the history of U.S.-Japanese relations remains an important one.

---

[7]The phrase used in the title of his earlier (October 1960) *Foreign Affairs* article criticizing U.S. policy in Japan.
[8]See Reischauer, *My Life Between Japan and America*, pp. 308, 340.
[9]*Ibid.*, p. 292.

STUDY/DISCUSSION QUESTIONS FOR
EDWIN O. REISCHAUER

1. What factors led to Reischauer's selection as U.S. Ambassador to Japan in 1961? What elements do you think made him a particularly strong choice for this position?

2. What were the particular problems in U.S.-Japanese relations which Reischauer had to deal with when he became ambassador in 1961? How successful was he in dealing with these matters?

3. What were Reischauer's views regarding U.S. military involvement in Vietnam in the mid-1960's? How did the Japanese view this issue?

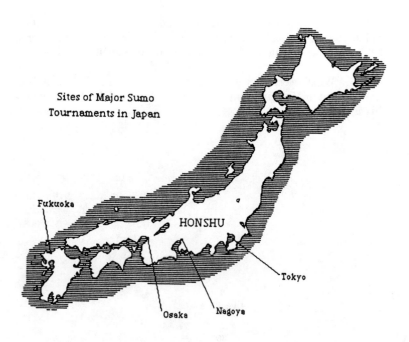

Sites of Major Sumo
Tournaments in Japan

Fukuoka

HONSHU

Tokyo

Osaka   Nagoya

Chapter 16

Baseball and Sumo

American Athletes in Japan-- and especially Jesse Kuhaulua ("Takamiyama"), First American Sumo Wrestler

Without a doubt the two most popular spectator sports in Japan today are sumo wrestling and baseball.[1] The first is a native sport whose origins extend back to ancient times; the second is a subtly (and sometimes unusually) modified version of the sport which began in the U.S. in the first half of the 19th century and has often been called the American "national pastime." In recent times (although for a longer period in baseball than in sumo) American athletes have been involved in both of these sports in Japan, often achieving spectacular results, but not without experiencing at the same time significant difficulties and frustrations. Their stories offer an interesting and sometimes dramatic study in cultural differences. This chapter looks briefly at the experiences of Americans in both sports, but focuses primarily on those of the first American (and non-Asian) to achieve success in

[1]Currently, professional soccer, introduced into Japan in the early 1990's, is the country's fastest growing spectator sport. The presence of large numbers of highly-paid foreign players on Japanese professional soccer teams will certainly add another interesting chapter to the history of foreign athletes in Japan in the years ahead.

Japanese sumo, the man known officially during his sumo career as Takamiyama Daigoro, but more often simply as "Jesse."

First, on the subject of baseball. The sport was initially introduced into Japan in the late 19th century and was played primarily at the high school and college levels, where by the turn of the century it had gained a considerable following. In 1936 the first professional league was organized after a number of famous American players, among them Babe Ruth and Lou Gehrig, had toured the country two years earlier. Interest at the professional level grew rapidly despite the harsh economic conditions of the depression era, and by 1940 there were a total of nine professional teams. The war years saw a falling off of interest, both because of the hardships of the times and the wartime leadership's feelings against Western culture, but it caught on again rapidly in the postwar period. Today there are two leagues-- the Pacific League and the Central League-- each comprised of six teams. Teams play a 130-game season, culminating in a "Japan Series" in October, and baseball is without question Japan's number one spectator sport.

Up to a point, the parallels with the sport as it is played in the U.S. are fairly obvious. The basic rules of play, the uniforms, the layout of the field, etc. are pretty much the same. Beneath the surface, however, key differences begin to appear. A number of these are outlined in a famous book by Robert Whiting entitled *The Chrysanthemum and the Bat; The Game Japanese Play* (1977). For one thing, the Japanese teams, with names such as the Yokohama Taiyo Whales, the Yakult Swallows and the Hiroshima Toyo Carp, are most often owned by businesses which utilize them primarily for public relations purposes. (The Hanshin Tigers, for example, are owned by a famous railroad line and department store in Osaka.) Vending stands at baseball stadiums in Japan sell *sushi* (rice cakes often featuring slices of raw fish), *ika* (dried squid) and *tako* (octopus) as well as traditional American hotdogs (known by their Japanese name, *hotto dogu*).[2] Television coverage, which typically begins an hour into the game, also ends at a predetermined time, so that the game must either be completed by listening to the radio or the results obtained from the late evening sports news. Games, after a certain point, can also end in a tie, a result which does not seem to bother the Japanese the way it would Americans who are willing to go on indefinitely to break one.

Differences between the way the game is played in the two countries become even more profound when viewed from the

---

[2] *Sake* (rice wine) is likewise just about as popular as beer (*biiru*) at Japanese ball parks.

perspective of foreign players engaged in the Japanese version of the sport. While Japanese baseball over the years has produced its own group of superstars-- the most famous being the power-slugging Oh Saduharu who in a career extending from 1959 to 1980 hit an amazing 868 homeruns!-- the era of the "economic miracle" and the soaring yen has seen the Japanese attempting increasingly to entice American stars to Japan. American players attempting to play the sport there encounter a unique set of problems, often reflecting deeper cultural differences.

First, of course, there is the training regimen. While American players practice extensively during spring training to 'get into shape,' and then do batting practice and fielding drills to get 'warmed up' before each game, the Japanese approach is a good deal more rigorous. Japanese teams maintain a difficult practice schedule which extends throughout much of the off-season as well as during the playing season itself, and embodies overall a kind of *samurai* (or *bushido*) ethic aimed at developing what is often referred to as "Fighting Spirit" (*faito* in Japanese). This process, in one player's account, consisted of nothing but running without ever touching a bat during the first ten days of spring training, then later included such activities as the "Thousand Ground Ball drill" in which a player is required to field ground balls nonstop for an hour, often leading to physical collapse requiring the administration of oxygen, or with the coaches continuing to hit balls aimed directly at the fallen player. Japanese players overall are taught to disregard their own personal safety for the good of the team-- an excellent example being the player who was given the "fighting spirit" award during the 1974 Japan Series for playing with a broken ankle.[3]

Differences of equal magnitude to the training regimen also exist in the actual playing of the game. Foreign players, coming to Japan with impressive reputations and expecting to set hitting and homerun records, are exposed to something known euphemistically as the "Floating Strike Zone," a process in which the superior strength of the foreigner is equalized by the Japanese umpire calling pitches strikes which are clearly outside of the strike zone. (American player Leon Lee quotes one umpire as telling him, "You are a foreigner and so strong and the Japanese pitchers need assistance against you."[4]) These and other efforts to "equalize" the abilities of foreign and Japanese players,

---

[3]See chapter 3, entitled "Baseball Samurai Style," in *The Chrysanthemum and the Bat* (Tokyo: Permanent Press, 1977) for a general discussion of Japanese training techniques, or Michael Shapiro's *Japan: In the Land of the Brokenhearted* (New York: Holt, 1989), pp. 96ff. for a specific account of American player Leon Lee's experiences in this regard.

[4]Quoted in *Japan: In the Land of the Brokenhearted*, pp. 95-6.

and to keep American players from dominating the sport, lead to obvious frustrations for the foreign players. Whiting's *The Chrysanthemum and the Bat* chronicles a number of the more celebrated, pre-1977 instances, among them the case of Daryl Spencer who was kept from winning a homerun championship in 1965 by an agreement among opposing pitchers to walk him every time he came to the plate.[5]

Apart from the obvious differences in size and strength between Japanese and American players, one finds deeper cultural differences reflected in the performance and playing styles as well-- Japanese players, while clearly better trained than their American counterparts, seem at the same time less creative in responding to unforeseen circumstances. Player Leon Lee, for example, recounts an incident where a Japanese player froze momentarily, and as a result fumbled a ground ball, when it bounced in a manner different from what he had been trained to expect.[6] [Similar observations regarding the Japanese have been made in other areas as well. In technical fields and industry, for example, Japanese workers often appear better trained and more reliable than their American counterparts. They are especially good at the *refinement* and *improvement* of existing processes, but at the same time appear less capable of coming up with totally new, 'breakthrough'-type discoveries.[7]] An inherent conservatism, aimed at avoiding "loss of face," also seems to permeate the Japanese approach to baseball strategy-- a point made in rather exaggerated fashion in the 1992 American movie, "Mr. Baseball," which depicts an American baseball player (Tom Selleck) trying to play the sport in Japan. Absolute dedication to one's work and placing it above all other considerations [another characteristic of workers generally in Japan] is reflected in the dismissal of Randy Bass, one of Japan's most popular foreign players in the late 1980's, when he elected against the orders of his team's management to accompany his seriously ill child back to the U.S. for treatment.

---

[5] See pp. 199-201; former N.Y. Yankee Joe Pepitone, who went to Japan to play in 1973 and spent most of his single season there faking injuries and generally causing trouble, serves to display the frustrations which often exist on the Japanese side in dealing with foreign players (see pp. 173-5).
[6] Described in *Japan: In the Land of the Brokenhearted*, pp. 100-1.
[7] See Sheridan M. Tatsuno, *Created in Japan: From Imitators to World-Class Innovators* (New York: Harper & Row, 1990) for an intriguing discussion of the subject of creativity from the standpoint of both cultures.

If Americans have experienced difficulties playing baseball in Japan, these problems have been mild in comparison to those which they have encountered attempting to break into Japan's other major spectator sport, sumo. Accounts of this sport go as far back in Japan as its first written histories, dating from the early part of the 8th century. A sport heavily laden with tradition, sumo often appears quite bizarre to Westerners. Enormous, seemingly out-of-shape wrestlers, sometimes weighing in excess of 500 pounds (in a country where obesity among the general population is much less common than in the U.S.), squatting and posturing on a raised clay platform, often for as long as five minutes, before finally colliding at the center of the ring-- then the encounter itself over almost before it starts (the average match lasts less than 90 seconds) with one of the participants either thrown down or off of the fighting space. 'Is that it?' the first-time spectator often gasps incredulously, as the wrestlers prepare to depart from the ring.

Actually, there is much more to Japanese sumo than what is seen at this first encounter. Wrestlers (known as *sumotori* or *rikishi* in Japanese), like Japanese baseball players, undergo a long and arduous training process. One important, and extremely painful aspect of the preparation, for example, is the *matawari*, in which the wrestler sits on the ground with his legs spread out as far as possible from his body, and then bends forward to touch his head on the ground. (In the early stages of a wrestler's training an older wrestler may lay across his back to 'facilitate' this process.) The squatting, leg-swinging and stomping movement (known as *shiko*), which constitutes another key warm-up activity, is likewise practiced vigorously-- a suggested 500 times a day for individuals planning to try out for the sport! The characteristic sumo shape, considered essential for the sport, is gained through the eating of an enormous bowl of stew (*chanko-nabe*) directly after the morning training session. This is usually followed by a nap to maximize the effects of the nourishment. Sumo training is obviously directed at the specific requirements of the sport-- power, strength, size, agility-- and such aspects as long-term endurance are given less consideration. Wrestlers nearly always become extremely winded after even the shortest match, and when a bout goes beyond the normal 90 seconds one finds both contestants panting heavily and unable to speak for several minutes after the encounter. (The life span of sumo wrestlers as a result of all this is considerably shorter than average.)

Because of its long history and connections with the Shinto religion, sumo has a number of quasi-religious rituals connected with it. Participants throw handfuls of salt before the bout to purify the ring, drink a special water (known as *chikara-mizu*), and wear long hair drawn up into a topknot (*mage*) and a special loincloth or belt (known as the *mawashi*). Referees also wear a traditional, very colorful and ornate costume. Wrestlers are ranked according to an elaborate ranking system with the highest rank being that of *yokozuna*, or Grand Champion, of which there may be several at one time (or none if no current wrestler is deemed worthy of the ranking).

Major sumo tournments (called *basho*) occur six times a year-- three times at Tokyo, alternating with three other major cities, Osaka, Nagoya and Fukuoka-- and last for a period of fifteen days. Wrestlers fight once a day during this period. The top wrestlers begin the tournament by competing against lesser wrestlers, but as the tournament proceeds they move progressively upward, until on the final days the top wrestlers fight against each other. The wrestler with the best overall record wins the tournament, with a playoff on the final day if two or more individuals have identical records. Television coverage of sumo tournaments begins each day in the early afternoon, when the lowest ranked wrestlers compete, and ends at six o'clock after the day's top matches.

With this basic understanding of the sport, and especially the awareness of its unique and highly-traditional character, one might imagine the chances of a foreigner successfully competing in it to be close to nonexistent-- and yet in recent years foreigners *have* achieved great success in Japanese sumo. Much of this is a result of the remarkable career of one individual, Jesse James Walani Kuhaulua, known during his wrestling career as Takamiyama.

Jesse Kuhaulua was born in Happy Valley on the Hawaiian island of Maui on June 16th, 1944. Even at birth he demonstrated the size (10 pounds, 14 ounces) which was to contribute greatly to his later success in sumo. His early life was marked by hard work, poverty and continued amazing growth in physical stature-- by the time he entered junior high school he was 5'11" and weighed 260 pounds! Despite an accident, suffered in the sixth grade, in which both of his legs were broken, he became a star football player in high school. Continuing problems with his legs, however, led him during his high school years to join a local sumo club (the sport had a considerable following in Hawaii because of the large Japanese-American population there), and it was as a member of this group that he was first seen by a touring Japanese sumo coach. The coach immediately saw the possiblities of a career in sumo for the well-built young Hawaiian, and convinced a well-known sumo stable in Japan to give him a chance to compete.

Up until this time no individual of non-Asian background had successfully competed in the sport at the professional level in Japan. Jesse arrived in Japan in February of 1964, homesick and without knowing a single word of Japanese. Many problems lay ahead. Unused to the cold of a Japanese winter he suffered greatly in the unheated training quarters of his sumo stable. Consumption of the training stew, which contained large quantities of fish (which he disliked), was also difficult. In addition, there were the rigors of the training itself, the painful *matawari* (described above), the endless repetitions of the *shiko*, the training practice of *teppo* (slapping a training pole until one's hands are bruised and sore), and, of course, the actual training bouts, in which the young aspirant was expected to face a steady stream of opponents, one after another, in the ring. Any letdown in the pace of any of these activities would result in several whacks across the back or legs from a trainer using a split-bamboo stick called a *shinai*, or, for more serious infractions, a senior wrestler might rub salt into his eyes or force a handful of dirt into his mouth. In his spare time, as a wrestler at the lowest level of development, he was also forced to do a daily round of chores which, for Jesse, included serving as a personal servant (*tsukebito*) to the stablemaster-- preparing his food, helping him bathe, and running endless numbers of personal errands for him.

Jesse appeared in his first major tournament in Osaka in May of 1964. By that time he had already been given his sumo name Takamiyama (which means "High-View Mountain"). From this point he climbed steadily upward through the lower division rankings, reaching the rank of *juryo* (the lowest of the full-fledged, professional sumo ranks) in February of 1967. By December of 1967 he had attained the next (*makunouchi*) rank, and in March of the following year, won his first of a record twelve *kinboshi* (defeats of a Grand Champion). His meteoric rise continued in the early 1970's. He won his first overall tournament, the Nagoya *basho*, in July of 1972, and attained his highest ranking, that of *sekiwake* (the third highest sumo rank behind *ozeki* and *yokozuna*), in August of that same year. He remained active in the sport until February of 1985, when he finally retired after over twenty years as a sumo wrestler.

It was Takamiyama then, more than any other, who broke the path for other foreigners in the sport. Extremely popular throughout his career, he is even credited with helping to change the public image of sumo wrestlers in Japan-- eventually achieving fluency in the language, he became a well-known public celebrity, appearing frequently in commercials and as a guest on popular tv programs, which in turn led other sumo stars to follow in a similar direction. In 1974 he married a

Japanese, and in 1976, in the aftermath of a Sumo Association decision prohibiting non-Japanese citizens from purchasing the "elder stock" (*toshiyori-kabu*) necessary to remain active in the sport after retirement, he officially made application for Japanese citizenship. He became a full citizen of Japan in 1980.

After retiring, Takamiyama opened his own sumo stable and has been highly successful in that area of the sport as well. One of his proteges, a fellow Hawaiian named Chadwick George Haheo Rowan (sumo name Akebono), became the first foreigner to attain the highest sumo rank of *yokozuna* ("Grand Champion") in 1993. In between Takamiyama and Akebono, another extremely popular foreign sumo, Samoan Salevaa Atisanoe (sumo name Konishiki), became the first foreigner to reach the second highest rank of *ozeki*. (Konishiki, often weighing in at over 575 pounds, was also one of the heaviest of all sumo wrestlers.)

Although controversies surrounding the presence of foreigners in the sport surface occasionally in Japan,[8] the ground gained by Takamiyama is unlikely to be lost. In 1992 there were a total of thirty-seven foreigners, twelve of them Americans, active in Japanese sumo. This fact, along with the elevation of his protege, Akebono, to *yokozuna* the following year, causes Takamiyama's achievement within the sport to continue to grow in significance.[9]

---

[8]In 1992 Samoan sumo wrestler Konishiki reportedly stated in an interview that he had been denied promotion to *yokozuna* because of his foreign status. He later claimed not to have made the statement, and Akebono's achievement of that rank the following year would also seem to argue against its validity.

[9]For an account of Takamiyama's life and career up to the time of his retirement see Andrew Adams & Mark Schilling, *Jesse! Sumo Superstar* (Tokyo: The Japan Times, 1985); for the sport of sumo itself, as well as the history of foreigners in it, see Lora Sharnoff's *Grand Sumo; The Living Sport and Tradition* (New York: Weatherhill, Rev. ed., 1993), among others.

1. Takamiyama (on right) in action in 1975. (Photo: Kyodo News Service.)

2. Takamiyama (far right) with Samoan sumo wrestler Konishiki in 1983. (Photo: Kyodo News Service.)

STUDY/DISCUSSION QUESTIONS FOR
BASEBALL AND SUMO

1. What are the chief differences between the way baseball is played in the U.S. and the way it is played in Japan? In what ways do these differences reflect deeper cultural differences?

2. Are the complaints of Americans playing baseball in Japan justified, or should they just 'bite the bullet' and adapt to the way the Japanese play the sport?

3. What were the major obstacles which Jesse Kuhaulua ("Takamiyama") had to overcome in order to achieve success in Japanese sumo?

4. How would you answer the assertion, put forward by at least some Japanese, that foreigners ought not to be allowed into the sport of sumo?

5. Which sport, baseball or sumo, do you think is more difficult for a foreign athlete to play in Japan, and why?

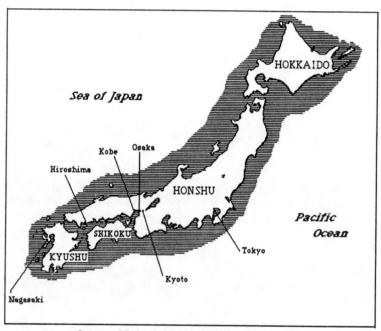

Japan: Main Islands and Cities (1930's)

Appendix I

The Decision to Attack Pearl Harbor: A Long-term View

I. Introduction

On the morning of December 7, 1941 the Japanese launched a surprise attack on the American naval base located at Pearl Harbor in the Hawaiian Islands. This act brought the United States into the Second World War and led ultimately to the defeat of Japan in August of 1945. Why did the Japanese launch this surprise attack? What did they hope to achieve by it? What are the underlying factors which serve to explain this decision? While various superficial answers to these questions can be given, the roots of this decision extend deep into the modern history of Japan and, in particular, into the long-term history of Japan's contact with the West. The purpose of this essay is to outline in somewhat more detail than one encounters in the usual U.S. history course the underlying causes for this fateful decision.

II. Japan's First Contact with the West

The first contact between Japan and the West occurred with the arrival in Japan of Portuguese traders and missionaries in the middle of the 16th century (the mid-1500's). This contact was a result of the same process of European expansion which brought Columbus and the Spanish westward to the New World. In the late 15th century (the late 1400's) the Portuguese had sought an alternate route to the Orient around the southern tip of Africa, and by the middle of the 16th century this process had brought them across the Indian Ocean and north to China and Japan.

Upon arriving in Japan the Portuguese encountered a people with a relatively high level of civilization. Since the middle of the 6th century, when the Japanese came under the direct cultural influence of China, they had developed their own written language; religion, especially **Buddhism**[1] (originally introduced from China), had flourished and undergone unique native developments; and literature, art and architecture had reached a considerable level of sophistication. Still, the exotic and distant culture of the Portuguese in the beginning at least presented an enormous attraction for the Japanese. At the heart of this foreign culture, of course, lay the Christian religion.

As in the case of the Spanish in the New World, Catholic missionaries accompanied the Portuguese on their voyages. These missionaries, beginning with St. Francis Xavier in 1549, made a tremendous impact on Japan for the next half century. Churches and seminaries were established in the western part of the country (on the southern island of Kyushu and the western part of the main island of Honshu), and perhaps as many as 300,000 Japanese (out of a total population of 15 to 20 million) were converted to Christianity by the end of the 16th century. The city of Nagasaki on the western side of Kyushu (later the site of the dropping of the second atomic bomb during World War II) was an important center for this religious activity.

Toward the end of the 16th century and the beginning of the 17th century, other European countries also made contact with Japan. The Spanish arrived in the 1590's, followed by the Dutch and English in the early 1600's. Spain and Portugal, although both Roman Catholic countries, were nevertheless rivals, both in trade and missionary activity. As a result they competed with each other instead of working together. Competition was particularly strong among the religious orders associated with the two countries-- the Portuguese Jesuits and the Spanish Franciscans, Dominicans and Augustinians. The arrival of the Dutch and the English, both representing Protestant countries and bitter trade rivals of the Portuguese and the Spanish, further complicated the situation.

At the time that these countries were making their appearance in Japan, Japan itself was undergoing a significant change in its political

---

[1]Bold highlighting indicates items of particular significance for beginning-level students.

life. For over a hundred years, since the mid-15th century (the 1460's), Japan had been in a chaotic and disorganized state. At approximately the same time that the first Europeans arrived, a series of political leaders emerged who began the process of reunifying the country. The Europeans themselves aided, at least indirectly, in this process through the introduction of new technology, such as guns, which aided these leaders in their military victories. By the late 16th and early 17th centuries, however, the rivalries of the European countries and the perceived political threat of Christianity in Japan led the last of these Japanese leaders (Hideyoshi Toyotomi in the 1590's and Tokugawa Ieyasu in the first decade of the 17th century) to take steps to expel the missionaries and to prohibit the practice of Christianity. This led eventually to a policy of isolation whereby Japan, during the **Tokugawa** or **Edo Period** (lasting from the early 17th century to the second half of the 19th century), consciously sought to seal itself off from outside influences and cultures. By the 1630's Christianity was all but wiped out in Japan,[2] and all contact with European countries was officially ended. The only exception to this were the Dutch, who were allowed to maintain a small trading post on an island in Nagasaki harbor but whose activities were strictly regulated.

Japan then, from the early part of the 17th century (or roughly the time that the first English settlers were establishing Massachusetts in Colonial America) to the mid-19th century (just prior to the American Civil War), was almost completely sealed off from Western contact.

III. Perry and the Opening of Japan

The isolated, self-enclosed culture that was Tokugawa Japan was rudely interrupted in July of 1853 by a fleet of ships under the command of Commodore Matthew C. Perry of the United States.

---

[2]Some Japanese Christians, known as "hidden Christians," maintained their faith on a kind of underground basis, but the practice of the religion itself was strictly prohibited by the government. During the early part of the 17th century there were severe persecutions of both Japanese Christians and the European missionaries who tried to remain in Japan against the government decrees.

Perry came as a part of an official mission ordered by then President of the United States, Millard Fillmore. The chief purposes of this mission were to negotiate a commercial treaty with Japan and to get Japan to open at least some of its ports to American ships. There was also the matter of Japan's treatment of foreign sailors who were forced into Japanese waters by storms or shortages of supplies. It was not uncommon for these individuals to be captured and put in cages, in the words of one author "not unlike the circus cages in which wild animals are now confined," and placed on public display.

Perry's visit, like the arrival of the Portuguese traders in the 16th century, was a part of a larger process which saw the United States seeking to compete in the Far Eastern trade with other Western countries, particularly the British and the Russians. Britain by this time had largely replaced the Portuguese and the Dutch as the dominant Western power in the region. It had defeated China in the "Opium War" fought in the early 1840's and after that war had forced an "unequal" treaty on China obtaining special trading rights and political powers. Following the British initiative, the United States had enacted a similar treaty with China in 1844. The lucrative "China trade" thus brought both Britain and the U.S. into close proximity with nearby Japan. Russia, as a result of expansion westward across Siberia in the late 18th century, was also emerging as a key player in the region. Perry's mission to Japan in 1853 was by no means the first attempt to open that country to Western trade and influence. There had been a number of earlier, unsuccessful efforts by all three of these Western powers during the first half of the 19th century.

Perry's approach in 1853 was direct and to the point. He handed over a list of demands, stressing the items noted above, and indicated that he would return the following year for an answer. He then proceeded to the nearby island of Okinawa and to several other far eastern ports, before returning in February of 1854 to receive the Japanese reply. Faced with the superior military force of the American warships Japan had little choice but to give in to the American demands. The result was the **Treaty of Kanagawa** negotiated in Yokohama at the end of March. This treaty opened two ports (one to the southwest of Tokyo on the main island of Honshu, the other on the far northern island of Hokkaido) to the Americans, gave assurances regarding the treatment of American sailors, agreed to the arrival of an American ambassador, and granted "most-favored-nation" status to the

U.S. (meaning that any additional trade concessions granted to other Western nations would automatically be granted to the United States as well).

Within a year treaties similar to the Treaty of Kanagawa were negotiated with Japan by Great Britain, Russia and the Netherlands. These treaties, along with the more specific commercial treaties with the U.S. and other Western powers which followed, became known as the **"unequal treaties"** because they placed Japan in a clearly inferior or subordinate position in the treaty relationship. In addition to the "most-favored-nation" clause, which all of these treaties contained, they also placed restrictions on the tariffs (import taxes) which Japan could place on foreign imports and included the concept of "extraterritoriality" (meaning that the citizens of these foreign nations living in Japan were subject to the laws of their own country and not those of Japan). While these treaties were hardly unique-- they were patterned after the treaty system which the British had earlier forced on China-- they were nevertheless viewed as an affront by the Japanese and as evidence of their second-class status in relation to the Western countries which had imposed them.

By the middle of the 1860's the Western presence in Japan had expanded greatly. More ports had been opened, Yokohama, a former fishing village near Tokyo, and Kobe further to the west being among the most important. Both of these cities had rapidly growing foreign settlements by mid-decade. Japan now faced crucial decisions regarding its future.

IV. The Meiji Period and Modernization

The conditions imposed on Japan by the Western nations in the treaties which followed the arrival of Perry in 1853 reflect an emerging pattern of 19th century Western **imperialism**. During the years which followed, the nations of the West, adhering in many ways to the doctrine of **Social Darwinism**, saw it to be both right and natural for them to colonize less technically-advanced regions of the world for their own gain and benefit. It was a kind of "survival of the fittest" pattern among nations. This was the period when the British completed their empire which stretched around the globe, and when other Western countries, including the United States, established colonies in far-flung places.[3] Past cultural attainments had little to do with this process, since places like India and China, the founders of great world civilizations in the past, were as much the victims of Western imperialism as less-developed regions. Japan in the 1860's then faced a clear choice: it could either accept a kind of colonial status along the lines of that imposed by the Western powers on neighboring China, or it could seek somehow, and against enormous odds, to modernize and eventually become itself a world power. The Japanese, after a brief period of political disarray, chose the latter course.

At the time of Perry's arrival in 1853 Japan was governed by a political system known as the **Tokugawa Shogunate**. This system, under the rule of a military dictator or **shogun**, had been in effect since the early 17th century but by the early 19th century it was in a state of decline. The arrival of Perry served as a catalyst to its final collapse. When this government proved unable to deal effectively with the foreign threat, a group of leaders from the outlying areas of Japan, away from the capital of Edo (Tokyo), moved to assume control of the government. They did this by bringing the emperor, who traditionally lived in the old capital city of Kyoto and had played no real part in the governing of the country for centuries, to Edo and placing him in charge of the government. This process, which took place in 1868, was known as the **Meiji Restoration**, after the name of this particular emperor's reign.[4] Although more accurately described as a "revolution," this process of returning the emperor to power served to legitimize the process of political change, and the leaders of the movement were then able to set up a new government on his behalf.

---

[3]A good example of this would be the American annexation of the Philippines following the Spanish-American War in 1898, but one need only look at an old pre-World War map of Africa or Southest Asia to find such places as the *Belgian* Congo, *German* East Africa, *Italian* Somaliland, *French* Indochina, etc.

[4]When Japanese emperors take office an official name is given to their period of rule. When the individual dies, he is then known by this name. Thus this emperor, whose actual name was Mutsuhito, became known after his death as the emperor Meiji. In a similar fashion the emperor during World War II, Hirohito, who died in 1989 is now known as the Emperor Showa after the name used to designate his period of rule.

After initially hoping to expel the foreigners, the new leaders of the country soon realized the hopelessness of accomplishing this and embarked on a process of **modernization**. Foreign study missions were sent from Japan to Western countries to observe and study the inner workings of these countries, and Western experts in a variety of fields were brought to Japan. In an amazingly short period of time Japan was transformed from a predominantly rural agricultural economy into a modern industrial one. Society was transformed, the old rigid class structure was abolished, a modern educational system was established, and a political system, which created on the surface at least the semblance of democracy, was put into place with the writing of the **Constitution of 1889**. Along with these changes, the process of industrialization was accomplished without high levels of foreign investment, leaving Japan independent financially of foreign governments.

Along with the economic, social and political changes of the **Meiji Period,** which lasted from 1868 to 1912, Japan also took steps to develop a modern army and navy and to use its military force to acquire colonies and to build an empire. Possessing few natural resources other than the energy and vitality of its people, and little space for the expansion of its population, the development of an overseas empire was of particular importance for Japan.[5] In the mid-1890s Japan fought a war with China (the **Sino-Japanese War of 1894-95**). Victory in this war brought them, among other things, the island of Taiwan (called Formosa under Japanese rule) and the tip of the Liaotung Peninsula in southern Manchuria. The fact that Russia, France and Germany later forced the Japanese to give up some of what they had gained in this war,[6] however, provided clear evidence that Japan was still regarded by these countries as a less than equal partner in the game of imperial growth and expansion.

To rectify this problem, Japan in the early 20th century moved to form a military alliance with Great Britain (the **Anglo-Japanese Alliance of 1902**) and then used this alliance to fight and defeat Russia in the **Russo-Japanese War of 1904-05**. The Japanese victory in this war brought Japan the southern half of Sakhalin Island

---

[5]Unlike the United States, for example, which was blessed with an abundance of both space and resources.
[6]In particular their rights on the Liaotung Peninsula.

East Asia: 1930's

(located north of Hokkaido), and development rights in Manchuria and Korea. Japan formally annexed Korea, renaming it Chosen, in 1910. By 1911 Japan had successfully negotiated new commercial treaties with the United States, Great Britain, the Netherlands, France and Russia to replace the earlier "unequal treaties," thus providing a more equal status with these Western nations.

By the end of the Meiji Period then, Japan had accomplished what no other non-Western country had done before, it had both successfully resisted Western imperialism and in the process had positioned itself as an emerging world power.

V. The Taisho Period: World War I and the Early 1920's

The **Taisho Period** (1912-1926)[7] in Japanese history is marked by Japan's attempts to adjust to a changing world political scene in the years following the **First World War** (1914-1918), and by increased experiments with democracy, begun in a very tentative fashion with the Meiji Constitution in 1889.

Japan entered the First World War on the allied side, which included Great Britain, France and Russia (and eventually the United States), very shortly after the war began in August of 1914. Japan hoped to use its support of the allied cause to gain German territorial possessions in China and the Pacific and to generally strengthen its position in the region. Declining to send troops to the European front, they chose to use their naval power against Germany in the far east, and in the process took over German holdings in Shandong (Shantung) Province in China as well as the Mariana, Caroline, and Marshall Islands in the central Pacific. During the war, in 1915, Japan also issued the **Twenty-one Demands**, a series of demands on China designed to further strengthen its position there. Both China and the Western powers (including the United States) reacted strongly to these demands, forcing Japan to soften its position. Following the war Japan was a full participant (the only non-Western country to serve as an equal partner in this process) at the **Versailles Peace**

---

[7]Named after the reign of the Emperor Taisho who replaced the Emperor Meiji following the latter's death in 1912.

Conference. Under the terms of the peace settlement, Japan was allowed to keep the territories it had gained from Germany.

Japan thus came out of the First World War with both territorial gains and improved trading conditions in Asia. The war, however, brought with it a significant change in international outlook and values. Following the lead of President Wilson in his **Fourteen Points,** issued in 1918, **self-determination** gradually began to replace imperialism as the basis of international conduct. In providing a clear example of the earlier pattern of imperialism and territorial expansion, Japan's conduct during World War I gained for it a somewhat negative image on the international scene in the years following the war. From the Japanese perspective, this change in international rules once again seemed to favor the Western powers, who under the new system were allowed to keep the colonial empires they had amassed while prohibiting other, non-Western countries from continuing the competition.[8] Despite this change in values, and the perception by some Japanese that it favored the Western powers over Japan, Japan officially sought to adjust to this new direction during the early years of the postwar period. Japan, unlike the United States, joined the newly-formed **League of Nations** in 1920, and later participated in the **Washington Conference** sponsored by the U.S. in 1921-22 which sought to limit naval expansion in the Pacific. In the aftermath of the Washington Conference Japan also agreed to take steps to give up, gradually, the territory in the Shandong Province in China which it had gained from Germany during the war. This period in Japan's international relations is sometimes referred to as **"Shidehara diplomacy"** after it chief architect, Shidehara Kijuro, a strong supporter of the new "internationalism" and a central figure in Japan's foreign policy during this period.

The early 1920's, which saw the Japanese consciously attempting to improve their relations with the West, also marked the highwater mark of democracy under the 1889 Constitution. The lower (elected)

---

[8] At the same time that the Fourteen Points, overall, moved in the direction of this new international ideal, it should be noted that Point V., specifically, called for "[a] free, open-minded, and absolutely impartial adjustment of all *colonial claims*, based upon the strict observance of the principle that in determining all such questions of sovereignty the interests of the populations concerned must have equal weight *with the equitable claims of the Government whose title is to be determined*" (emphasis added.)

house of the Diet, which was established under that document, was initially chosen by only a little over 1% of the population. It played no role in the selection of the prime minister and cabinet (who were technically appointed by the emperor but were in actuality chosen by the small group of Meiji political leaders who ran the government from behind the scenes), and it had almost no decision-making powers. Over time the role of the Diet expanded, and the 1920's saw the passage of both a **universal manhood suffrage act** (1925), which gave all male citizens the right to vote, and experimentation with **"party government"** which gave the power to form a goverment (i.e., select a prime minister and cabinet) to the party holding the majority of seats in the Diet.

Altogether then, despite a certain amount of political turmoil resulting from the new democracy and a rapid rate of social change (Japan during this period had its own version of the "Roaring Twenties" complete with jazz music, mass culture and flappers), the early 1920's were a generally positive time in Japanese development. Unfortunately, forces existed both inside and outside of the country which would lead to darker times in the years ahead.

VI. Tensions Between the U.S. and Japan

Before proceeding to the specific series of events which brought Japan into the Pacific War it is useful to sketch out briefly the nature of Japan's long-term relationship with the U.S., and to note in particular the tensions which had existed over the years between these two countries.

Strains in U.S.-Japanese relations can be traced back to the middle of the 19th century. It was the United States and the arrival of Perry in 1853, after all, which had forced Japan into modernization. One can argue, of course, that if the U.S. had not done this, Great Britain or Russia would have. Still, Perry's arrival technically initiated the process. In addition, during the second half of the 19th century the United States (just emerging itself as a world power) and Japan became rivals in the Pacific. Both countries had their eyes on the Hawaiian Islands, for example, and Japanese interests there were clearly a factor underlying the U.S. decision to annex the Hawaiian chain in 1900. Both countries, likewise, had interests in China as noted earlier.

Another factor complicating U.S.-Japanese relations during this period was U.S. immigration policy and the racial attitudes underlying it. The period extending from the end of the American Civil War to the onset of World War I saw the greatest influx of immigrants in U.S. history. Often referred to as the **"New Immigration"** (because of the diversity of nationalities represented), immigration to the U.S. during this period was largely unrestricted. Almost anyone able to pass a simple medical exam was allowed to enter the country. The sole exception, beginning in 1882, were the Chinese. Because of labor disputes and racial tensions on the west coast, Congress passed the **Chinese Exclusion Act** in that year, placing a ten year hold on Chinese immigration. The Act was renewed ten years later and made permanent in the early years of the 20th century. This racial discrimination toward the Chinese was also extended to the Japanese. Although Japanese immigrated to the U.S. in fairly large numbers in the late 19th and early 20th centuries, they tended to be lumped together with the Chinese and other people of Oriental background in the popular imagination. There was much talk in both the U.S. and Canada at this time of the **"Yellow Peril"** in reference to the immigration of Oriental peoples. In California, where many Japanese settled, laws were passed denying Orientals, including Japanese, the right to own land, and placing their children in segregated schools. Tensions in this area led, during the presidency of Theodore Roosevelt, to the so-called **Gentlemen's Agreement** (1908) between the U.S. and Japan which all but eliminated Japanese immigration to the U.S., at a time when the immigration of Europeans to the U.S. from all parts of Europe continued unabated. These racial attitudes continued to be a sore spot in U.S.-Japanese relations in the years following World War I (when the U.S. refused to support a Japanese proposal to include a clause on "racial equality" in the Versailles Peace Treaty) and in the 1920's, when restrictive legislation embodied in the **Immigration Act of 1924**, specifically excluded the Japanese from immigration to the U.S.[9]

---

[9]Similar racial attitudes can be seem during the Second World War when thousands of Japanese-Americans living on the west coast of the U.S. were moved to relocation camps, and suffered large-scale confiscation of property, in the period following the Pearl Harbor attack. No comparable action occurred in connection with Americans of German ancestry and background.

Although there were more positive moments in U.S.-Japanese relations in the years prior to the 1930's, such as the role played by Theodore Roosevelt in mediating the peace settlement following the Russo-Japanese War in 1905 or U.S. aid to the victims of the Great Tokyo Earthquake in 1923, the long-term history of competition in the Pacific region and the nature of racial attitudes in the U.S. during these years clearly played a role in the events which were to follow.

VII. The Depression and the Rise of the Military

The world-wide Depression which began in the United States following the **Stock Market Crash** in 1929 had already begun in Japan in 1926-27. In these years the Japanese economy experienced a slowdown and many banks failed much as they did during this same period in the U.S. In the years after the Stock Market Crash the effects of the Depression in Japan became catastrophic. Exports fell 50% between 1929 and 1931. Worker income and the price of agricultural products fell dramatically. As in the U.S., Japanese farmers were particularly hard hit, with many reduced to eating the bark of trees or selling their female children to avoid starvation. In the midst of this economic collapse the experiments with party government and democracy which had marked the early years of the 1920's were discredited, and certain basic flaws in the political system created under the Meiji Constitution (in particular the independence of the military and its separation from civilian control) began to surface.

The military itself was divided into two groups. One group, comprised largely of senior officers, favored a moderate course, while the other, comprised of younger officers (many of them from rural areas who had gone into the military to avoid the devastating effects of the collapsing rural economy), favored a more radical solution to the Depression through militarism and foreign expansion. These younger officers embarked on a series of "independent actions," both domestic, attempting to overthrow the civil government,[10] and foreign, initiating

---

[10]Two attempts to overthrow the government, both seeking to utilize the earlier pattern of political change in Japan by claiming to act in the name of the emperor, were made by members of the younger officer group, in May of 1932 and February of 1936. Both attempts were put down by the more

acts of aggression in Manchuria in 1928 and 1931 and with China in 1937, none of which were planned or even fully anticipated by the central government.

VIII. Aggression in Manchuria and China

The action of the military in Manchuria in 1931 is usually identified in the standard accounts of the Second World War as a crucial event leading up to the war. It is important to note, however, that this action did not mark either the beginning of the Japanese presence in that area or the first "independent action" undertaken by the Japanese military there.

The Japanese presence in Manchuria extended back to the Sino-Japanese War of 1894-95 and was greatly strengthened by the Japanese victory in the war with Russia ten years later. As a result of that latter conflict, Japan's economic rights in Manchuria were formally recognized, and in the years that followed the area became a focal point of Japanese overseas development. (By the late 1920's 75% of the foreign investment in Manchuria was Japanese, approximately 40% of Japan's crucial China trade occurred specifically with that region, and as many as a million Japanese subjects (a large percentage of them Koreans) were residing there.) In the mid-1920's the growth of the **Chinese Nationalist Movement** under Chiang Kai Shek to the south, and fears regarding the expansion of the Soviet Union, which also had long-standing economic interests in Manchuria, began to present a threat to Japanese interests there. It was this, coupled with the onset of the Depression and the rise of "the younger officer problem," which led to the first independent action of the military in the region. In 1928 the Japanese army in Manchuria, acting completely on its own without orders from the Tokyo government, assassinated a local leader, Chang Tso-lin, who was proving uncooperative to Japanese officials. The incident, which brought the downfall of the existing government in

---

conservative military faction. The process, however, which provided further evidence of the weakness of the civil government, served to give increased power to the military overall.

Tokyo, was a clear precursor to what was to occur in more highly-publicized fashion three years later.[11]

The 1931 incident, like the earlier act, was undertaken without either the knowledge or approval of the home government. Faced with growing difficulties in the region, the government had resolved to come to a conclusion regarding the Manchurian question by the spring of 1932. Instead, the military, acting on its own, created an incident in September of 1931 which allowed them to take over the region. In September of 1932, reacting to what the military had already initiated, the Tokyo government proceeded to turn Manchuria into the puppet state of "Manchukuo." It was this situation which served to ignite international opinion against Japan in the early 1930's. When the League of Nations, in 1933, took steps to condemn Japan's action, Japan formally withdrew from that body.

The incident which initiated war with China in 1937 had much the same type of beginning. Fear of both the Chinese Nationalist and Soviet threats to Japanese interests in China had led to some discussion of the use of military force to deal with the situation by the Japanese government, but this was still very much a "minority" viewpoint when fighting broke out, largely by accident, between Chinese and Japanese forces in the vicinity of Peking on July 7, 1937. The full-scale war which followed proved devastating for the Japanese in several regards. In terms of public opinion-- especially following the **"Rape of Nanking"** in December of 1937 in which Japanese forces unleashed a rampage of murder and destruction on the civilian population of that city-- it marked another significant step down in Japan's relations with the West. At the same time, by creating a tremendous drain on Japanese resources, it led Japan, as subsequent events unfolded, into further acts of military aggression.

IX. Collision Course with the U.S. and the Growth of the German Alliance

---

[11]Rather interestingly, the Japanese emperor at this time (Emperor Hirohito) took steps to condemn this incident and to have the perpetrators punished. His commands, however, were not followed.

The outbreak of war with China in 1937 clearly placed Japan on a collision course with the U.S. With long-standing interests in China, both economic as well as moral (China had been an important arena for the missionary activities of American churches since the 19th century), the United States felt obliged to do everything possible (short of war at this point) to turn back Japanese aggression. At the same time that relations with the U.S. worsened, Japan moved to strengthen its relationship with Germany.

Germany's attraction for Japan extended back to the 19th century. As a part of the modernizations of the Meiji Period Japan had looked to Germany, itself a newly emerging state at that time, as a model in at least two areas. One was in the organization and development of its army, and the other was in the writing of its 1889 constitution, which, as has been noted, presented difficulties for the development of democracy in Japan because of the independent status it granted to the military forces. In the years following World War I (when Japan had of course fought on the Allied side against the Germans), Japan had gravitated back toward Germany as a possible ally against Soviet expansion in Manchuria. In 1936 Japan signed the **Anti-Comintern Pact** with Germany pledging mutual support against the spread of communism. During this period too, Germany, under the leadership of Adolph Hitler who came to power in 1933, was preparing to embark on its own course of military aggression and expansion.

The **Nazi-Soviet Pact of 1939** in which Germany entered into a non-aggression pact with the Soviet Union, much to the surprise and dismay of Japan, brought a temporary downturn in German-Japanese relations. In the early months of 1940 a moderate government which came to power briefly in Japan[12] sought to improve relations with Great Britain and the United States, but the inflexibility of these countries regarding Japan's position in China led to the collapse of that government. With the U.S., in particular, threatening economic sanctions against Japan unless it undertook an immediate withdrawal of its troops from China, Japan responded by moving its army into the northern part of French Indochina[13] on September 23, 1940. The U.S. reacted three days later by announcing an embargo on scrap iron

---

[12]The government of Admiral Yonai which lasted from January to July.

[13]The countries of Vietnam, Laos and Cambodia were at that time a part of the French colonial empire.

shipments to Japan, and on September 27th Japan signed the **Tripartite Treaty** with Germany and Italy, formalizing its alliance with the Axis powers and taking another major step toward war.

Why did Japan proceed in this fashion in the fall of 1940, especially given the economic sanctions threatened by the U.S. and the demonstrated unreliability of Germany as an ally? First of all, on the U.S. side of the equation, threats of economic embargo had the unintended effect of pushing the Japanese into further expansion rather than serving to curtail it. Since the continued presence in China was seen to be vital to Japanese interests, new sources of raw materials critical to the war effort there were needed to replace those being cut off by the United States. In addition, U.S. ultimatums to Japan in regard to China at this time seemed basically out of touch with the views of the American people regarding war. Since the mid-1930's the U.S. Congress had passed a series of acts, known as the **Neutrality Acts** (1935-39), designed to keep the U.S. out of international conflicts. The election campaign underway in the U.S. in the fall of 1940 also stressed non-involvement in "foreign wars." From this the Japanese read a lack of popular support for military action in the U.S.

As to the matter of Germany, despite evidence of past unreliability, the German alliance offered several things to Japan at this juncture. First, one need only consider the conditions in Europe at this time. By the late summer of 1940 Germany had completed its sweep across France and the low countries and was in the process of subjecting Britain to the large-scale aerial bombardment known as the **"Battle of Britain."** Germany clearly appeared dominant on the European continent. Through an alliance with Germany and the likely German defeat of the former European powers, Japan would be in a position to take over the Asian colonies of these defeated nations. In addition, the Nazi-Soviet Pact, surprising as it may have been to the Japanese the year before, nevertheless offered the possibility of achieving a solution to the Soviet threat through the use of German mediation.[14] Finally, of course, the existence of the Tripartite Treaty, which carried with it the agreement that Germany and Italy would

---

[14]Even though the Germans abrogated their pact with the Soviets the following June, and invaded Russia, Japan did negotiate a non-aggression pact with the Soviets in the spring of 1941 which lasted until the last days of the war.

automatically go to war with any country which declared war on Japan, meant that should the U.S. declare war on Japan, Japan would not be in it alone. The U.S. would be engaged in a war on two separate fronts.

All of these factors then help to explain Japan's willingness to risk the anger of the U.S. through further expansion in the fall of 1940, as well as its decision made at the same time to strengthen its ties with Germany. This same set of factors a year later would underlie the fateful decision to attack Pearl Harbor.

X. Pearl Harbor

The attack on Pearl Harbor in December of 1941, unlike the Manchurian and China incidents earlier, was planned at the highest levels of the Japanese government. In July of 1941 Japanese troops had moved into the southern part of Indochina, and in response the U.S. had enlarged its trade embargo to include oil, which was, of course, a vital resource for Japanese military operations. The Japanese by this time had also taken steps to mask continued aggression in southeast Asia by the creation of the **Greater East Asia Co-Prosperity Sphere**, claiming in effect that their expansion was creating a new economic and political order in the region as well as serving to "liberate" these areas from Western domination.[15] By the late autumn of 1941 another moderate government, with some inclination toward improving relations with the U.S., had come and gone,[16] and the militarists were in control in Tokyo. Planning now moved forward for the Pearl Harbor attack.

As we have seen, a number of factors contributed to the decision to attack the U.S. The knowledge that due to the Tripartite Treaty the United States, once it declared war on Japan, would also be at war with

---

[15]While there is, of course, some small degree of truth in this claim, since many of these areas were under the control of Western countries at that time, the end result of Japanese action entailed the replacement of one form of colonial control with another.

[16]The third government of Prince Konoe which lasted from July to October of 1941. Konoe during this period desperately sought a meeting with President Roosevelt in an attempt to reach some accommodation between the U.S. and Japan. The meeting never took place, and Konoe was replaced as prime minister by General Tojo, a hard-line militarist, in October.

Germany and Italy was part of it. The misreading of the likely American response to such an attack-- the apparent aversion to war reflected in American public opinion and foreign policy decisions during the 1930's-- also played a role. In addition, Japan looked back to its earlier history and in particular to the war with Russia in the first decade of the century where an alliance with a major European power (Great Britain) and a surprise attack against the Russian navy (the day before war was formally declared) had proven highly successful. Never expecting to defeat the U.S. outright, Japan's plan was to strike a devastating blow, force the U.S. into an unpopular war fought on two fronts simultaneously, and then to work for a **negotiated settlement** in which at least some of their "rights" in China and other parts of southeast Asia would be recognized. Their strategic position in the Pacific, so much closer to the theater of action (and to the critical resources of the region) than was the U.S., also served to strengthen their resolve. Few of the Japanese policy-makers responsible for the decision to attack Pearl Harbor anticipated the effect that the attack would have on public opinion and support for the war in the U.S., nor did they expect that **unconditional surrender** would become the terms of the war the U.S. would wage against them. Pearl Harbor proved to be a tragic miscalculation for Japan.

XI. Conclusion

At this point we end the account. The portions of the story which follow-- the course of the war itself and the eventual surrender of Japan following the use of the atomic bomb on Hiroshima and Nagasaki in August of 1945-- can easily be filled in from any standard U.S. history text. The purpose of this account has been to examine the factors underlying the Japanese decision to attack Pearl Harbor from a long-term perspective, to attempt to understand both *why* and *how* this decision was reached. The account has been a rather lengthy one, extending over nearly four hundred years of Japanese history and including a number of topics that on the surface may seem to have little to do with the event it is leading up to. Still, there are larger forces at work here which need to be recognized. One needs to develop, for example, a sense of Japan's perspective as it encountered the Western "threat" in the years following the arrival of Commodore Perry in the 19th century, and to see Japan as an "outsider" attempting to come to grips with the Western way of acting and behaving as a world power, particularly as the rules governing that action changed in the years following the First World War. At the same time, one needs to realize that many of the Western social and political ideals-- the very idea of democracy itself, for example-- were new and alien concepts to the Japanese, which in turn needed to be experimented with and applied to their own needs and situation, with sufficient time and the right conditions for this development to take place.[17] Perhaps a better understanding of the Japanese perspective on the part of the Western Allies in the years leading up to World War II would have lead to a different outcome than Pearl Harbor and the devastation of the Pacific phase of the war. Certainly missed opportunities and gross misreadings of each other's motives and outlooks existed on both sides. While this discussion makes no attempt to exonerate Japan for its actions in the period leading up to the war, it *does* argue for the need to develop fuller understandings among nations. To deal successfully with international conflicts in the future we must seek to understand more fully the perspective and outlook of our adversaries, and there is no way to accomplish this other than through the in-depth study of their history and culture. A better understanding of Japanese history and culture on the part of U.S. policy-makers in the period leading up to World War Two *might* have led to a different outcome. Certainly it wouldn't have made things any worse.

Further Reading

The following standard histories of Japan contain fuller discussions of the material outlined above:

W.G. Beasley, *The Rise of Modern Japan* (1990)

Edwin O. Reischauer, *Japan: The Story of a Nation*, 4th ed. (1990)

---

[17]One need only consider the success of democracy in Japan as it developed out of the postwar Occupation to see the basic truth of this statement.

Edwin O. Reischauer & Albert M. Craig, *Japan: Tradition & Transformation*, Rev. ed. (1989)

Richard Storry, *A History of Modern Japan* (1984)

John E. Wiltz's *From Isolation to War, 1931-1941* (1968) (especially chapters 2 and 5) offers a good, brief account of the diplomatic relations between the United States and Japan during this critical period.

Appendix II

Chronology of Events from the Arrival of Commodore Perry to the Japanese Attack on Pearl Harbor and the U.S. Entry into the Pacific War

1853
Arrival of Commodore Perry in Japan
1861-5
U.S. Civil War
1868
Meiji Restoration - new government in Japan pledges itself to modernization
1877
Satsuma Rebellion successfully put down in Japan
(Late 19th century)
Both the U.S. and Japan undergo rapid industrialization and urbanization
1894-5
Sino-Japanese War; Japan acquires Taiwan
1898
Spanish-American War; U.S. acquires Puerto Rico, Guam, the Philippines; annexes Hawaii
1904-5
Russo-Japanese War; Japan acquires southern half of Sakhalin Island, development rignts in Korea and Manchuria
1908
"Gentlemen's Agreement" - Japan agrees to curtail immigration to the U.S. in response to U.S. fears of "Yellow Peril"
1910
Japan formally annexes Korea

1914-9

Japan fights on Allied side in WWI, but seeks to gain former German territory at the end of the war in violation of Wilson's Fourteen Points

(Early 1920's)

"Roaring Twenties" in the U.S.; period of "Taisho Democracy" in Japan

1926-7

Beginning of economic depression in Japan

1928

Assassination of Chinese warlord, Chang Tso-lin, by Japanese military in Manchuria

1929

Stock Market Crash in U.S.

1930

Hawley-Smoot Tariff passes in the U.S. - raises tariff rates to an all-time high, severely restricting foreign trade

1931

Sept. - "Manchurian Incident" - Japanese army moves to occupy Manchuria

1932

Jan. - U.S. Sec. of State Stimson formally announces "Nonrecognition Policy" in regard to Japan's action in Manchuria

May - "5-15 Incident" - 1st attempted coup by "younger officer" element in Japanese military; Prime Minister Inukai assassinated

June - Joseph Grew arrives in Tokyo as new U.S. Ambassador

Sept. - Japan creates puppet state of Manchukuo

Nov. - Franklin Roosevelt elected President of the U.S.

1933

Mar. 4 - Roosevelt inaugurated; New Deal begins in the U.S.
Mar. 24 - Adolf Hitler assumes dictatorial powers in Germany
Mar. 27 - Japan formally withdraws from the League of Nations in response to the Lytton Commission report condemning Japanese aggression in Manchuria

(1935-9)

Neutrality Acts passed in the U.S. to keep the U.S. out of international conflicts

1936

Feb. - "2-26 Incident" - 2nd major coup attempt by "younger officer" element in Japanese military

Nov. - Japan signs Anti-Comintern Pact with Germany

1937

July - "China Incident" - war between Japan and China begins

Dec. - U.S.S. *Panay* sunk; "Rape of Nanking" by Japanese troops

1938

Nov. - "New Order in East Asia" (forerunner of "Greater East Asia Co-Prosperity Sphere") proclaimed by government of Prince Konoe

1939

July - U.S. notifies Japan of termination of 1911 commercial treaty, sets stage for later embargoes

Aug. - Nazi-Soviet Pact

Sept. 1 - Germany invades Poland; WWII begins in Europe

1940

Jan.-July - Moderate government of Admiral Yonai

July - Return to power of Prince Konoe

Aug. - Japanese Foreign Minister Matsuoka proclaims "Greater East Asia Co-Prosperity Sphere"

Sept. 23 - Japanese troops move into northern Indochina

Sept. 26 - U.S. places embargo on vitally-needed scrap iron shipments to Japan

Sept. 27 - Tripartite Treaty signed between Germany, Italy and Japan

1941

Apr. - Non-aggression pact between the Soviet Union and Japan

June - Germany invades the U.S.S.R.

July 25-6 - Japanese troops move into southern Indochina; U.S. freezes Japanese funds, extends embargo to oil

Aug.-Sept. - Konoe seeks meeting with Roosevelt

Oct. - Konoe government falls; replaced by government of Gen. Tojo

Dec. 7 - Japanese attack Pearl Harbor

Dec. 8 - U.S. declares war on Japan

Appendix III

Anti-Japanese Sentiments in Recent American Popular Fiction[1]

I. The state of American popular culture regarding Japan

Sheila K. Johnson in *The Japanese Through American Eyes* (Stanford University Press, 1988) traces the history of attitudes regarding the Japanese in American popular culture since the end of World War II. In this work she finds a shift from the anti-Japanese propaganda of the wartime period to a more romanticized, positive view of Japan in the early postwar years and back to a more negative view (on the part of at least a certain segment of the American population) in the light of growing economic tensions in the 1980's. What is the current state of American popular culture on this subject?

As one might imagine in looking at a subject this complex and varied in character one continues to observe a wide range of attitudes. Reading newspaper editorials written in the U.S. at the time of President Bush's 1991 trip to Japan (without actually having counted or tallied them) one seemed to see about as many editorials attacking Japan-bashing and attributing American economic woes to its own business practices as those critical of Japanese policies. An American television movie dealing with the dropping of the atomic bomb on Hiroshima which aired on the 45th anniversary of that event in the summer of 1990 (NBC's "Hiroshima: Out of the Ashes") was highly sympathetic to the plight of the Japanese, and the treatment of the Japanese in the seemingly endless number of feature stories dealing with the 50th anniversary of Pearl Harbor in the U.S. in the fall of 1991 were far more balanced than one might have expected.

[1]This article, written by the author, originally appeared in *International Studies* [a journal published by the International Studies Association of Osaka Gakuin University, Osaka, Japan], Vol. 4, No. 2 (December 1993), pp. 75-91. Reprinted with the permission of Osaka Gakuin University.

Despite these positive signs, however, other areas of U.S. popular culture, and in particular a number of recent works of bestselling fiction, have been marked by a more negative direction. In this regard, the end of the Cold War and the disappearance of the Soviet Union as the traditional adversary in American action/adventure literature has found the authors of at least some of these works turning to the Japanese as a source of villains.

This essay will focus on one recent example of this new body of popular fiction, Clive Cussler's 1990 bestseller, *Dragon*. Before doing so, however, it is worth noting that the phenomenon of anti-Japanese sentiments can be observed in a number of recent non-fiction bestsellers in the U.S. as well. One need only look at such works as Pat Choate's *Agents of Influence* (Knopf, 1990), in which the author sets out to attack the lobbying practices of foreign governments in the U.S.,[2] but then proceeds to use Japan as the sole example (the work is subtitled "How Japanese Lobbyists in the United States Manipulate America's political and Economic System"), or *The Second Pearl Harbor* (National Press), published on the 50th anniversary of Pearl Harbor in December of 1991, in which American business tycoon T. Boone Pickens and others respond in a highly-charged manner to the controversial Japanese bestseller, Shintaro Ishihara's *The Japan That Can Say No* (English translation, Simon and Schuster, 1991). (A line from the "Preface" to *The Second Pearl Harbor* reads: "The intent of this book is to shock the American public into realizing that that we are at war with Japan."[3]) A final example of a non-fiction work of this type that might be mentioned here is George Friedman and Meredith Lebard's *The Coming War with Japan* (St. Martin's, 1991), which predicts a real war (as opposed to an economic one) between the U.S. and Japan within the next twenty years.

II. The portrayal of the Japanese as villains in Clive Cussler's *Dragon*

Clive Cussler's 1990 bestseller *Dragon* makes an interesting case study in the use of the Japanese as villains in post-Cold War American popular fiction. Clive Cussler (b. 1931) is well established in the U.S.

---

[2]See pp. xiii and xxii.

[3]T. Boone Pickens et al., *The Second Pearl Harbor* (Washington, D.C.: National Press, 1991), p. 13. A similar, although slightly more balanced response to Ishihara's work can be found in Leon Anderson's *Japanese Rage; Japanese Business and Its Assault on the West* (Four Walls Eight Windows, 1992).

as the author of a number of popular novels pitting his larger-than-life American hero, Dirk Pitt, against villains representing a variety of different nationalities. (Three of his works utilize Soviet villains, others, prior to the publication of *Dragon*, have used ex-Nazis, South Africans, Arab and Mexican terrorists, and even the British (*Night Probe!* - 1981) as the principal foes.) In *Dragon* it is Japan and the Japanese that present the threat which his hero must overcome.

The specific threat in *Dragon* comes not from the Japanese government itself but from an underground group within the country which has devised a plot (known as the Kaiten Project) by which they hope to hold the major economic powers of the world hostage through the smuggling of nuclear warheads hidden in automobiles into their countries. Capable of being detonated from a secret control center in Japan, the bombs are to be located in sparsely-populated areas but will serve, when set off, to create "an electromagnetic pulse" which will rise into the atmosphere and erase the memories of all the country's computers, in effect destroying its entire communications and data-storage network.[4] The book recounts how Dirk Pitt and his fellow operatives drawn from the U.S. and British intelligence services manage to thwart this plot and destroy its leaders. The heroes ultimately use a lost atomic bomb from World War II which lies in a wrecked plane on the ocean floor off the coast of Japan to destroy the Kaiten Project's command center. The bomb creates a *tsunami* or "seismic sea wave," which causes the island containing the command center to disappear into the sea.[5]

The negative portrayal of Japanese in the novel encompasses a wide range of characters, beginning with the unstable Mr. Yamada, an "important company director," who has a "hysterical outburst" and probable "nervous breakdown" when problems occur on a ship which is bringing some of the cars with nuclear warheads to the the U.S.,[6] and extending to the darkly villainous depiction of the plot's chief perpetrators. Among the latter are Hideki Suma, the Kaiten Project's main instigator and planner. In line with the numerous racial stereotypes the novel employs in its characterizations, he is described as being rather short by "Western standards" but tall "by Japanese ideals" at 170 centimenters, with white hair replacing the "black mane common to almost all Japanese men and women." His most important

---

[4]Clive Cussler, *Dragon* (New York: Simon and Schuster, 1991), pp. 292-3, 365.
[5]*Ibid.*, pp. 518-20, 479.
[6]*Ibid.*, p. 35.

physical characteristic are his blue eyes, the "legacy, possibly, of an
early Dutch trader or English sailor," an example of racial mixing
which seems to render him all the more capable of villainy. While not
terribly bright (he makes the usual mistakes which lead to the collapse
of his evil designs), he is a complete pragmatist in the pursuit of his
ends, rejects traditional Japanese culture and values (although he is
willing to exploit the *samurai* ethic still present in his assistant, Moro
Kamatori), and emits a sound like "the hiss of a viper" when he is
angry.[7]

Kamatori, Suma's assistant, possesses even more completely the
physical characteristics of a villain. Two brief and somewhat
contradictory descriptions, taken from different points in the novel,
serve to serve to highlight his physical appearance and character:

> Kamatori had a stolid, resolute face flanked by
> oversized ears. Beneath heavy black brows, the dark
> lifeless eyes peered through a pair of thick-lensed rimless
> glasses. *No smile ever crossed his tight lips.* He was a man
> without emotions or convictions.

>   *   *   *

> Moro Kamatori didn't merely look evil, he was evil.
> The pupils of his eyes never changed from the violent
> black poisonous stare, and *when the tight lips parted in a
> smile*, which was seldom, they revealed a set of teeth laced
> with more gold than the Mother Lode.[8]

Kamatori is, of course, totally loyal to Hideki Suma and his plan
for world economic domination, and as further evidence of the evil he
represents, he keeps the heads of some thirty individuals who he has
personally killed in the pursuit of their evil schemes mounted as
trophies on the walls of his study. He is eventually killed by Dirk Pitt
is a sword battle, despite the fact that he is an expert in *kenjutsu*
swordsmanship, and left impaled by a saber through the groin on the
wall next to his trophies.[9]

Among other Japanese villains in the novel are: two young
Japanese-Americans (George Furukawa and Roy Orita) who have grown

---

[7]*Ibid.*, pp. 139, 203, 204, 422.
[8]*Ibid.*, pp. 140, 373 (emphasis added).
[9]*Ibid.*, pp. 374, 398.

up in the U.S. but turn against their adopted country to spy for Suma Industries; Korori Yoshishu, the head of the Gold Dragons, an infamous Japanese crime organization from which Hideki Suma also traces his roots; and Ichiro Tsuboi, the director of a powerful Japanese securities company, who is secretly involved in the Kaiten Project and tries at one point to blackmail the U.S. government.[10] Even the prime minister of Japan at the time of the plot, while not directly involved in its planning and execution, is accused by the Americans of being aware of its existence and is forced to resign under threat of an American trade boycott.[11]

Not all of the Japanese in the novel are evil of course-- there is a Japanese-American agent (Jim Hanamura) who remains loyal to the U.S. (and pays for his loyalty with his life when he is brutally beheaded by Moro Kamatori)-- but even positive characterizations are often marked by blatant racial and cultural stereotypes. A typical example is the case of the "[w]illowy" and long-legged Toshie Kudo, Suma's personal sectretary and mistress. She is the daughter of an impoverished fisherman who was forced to sell her to Suma in order to get money to buy a new fishing boat. She eventually comes over to the American side and becomes involved in a relationship with Al Giordino, Dirk Pitt's friend and associate, taking her place in a long line of Oriental women in American popular fiction who prove attractive to Western males because they possess physical traits considered uncharacteristic of their race-- along with the long legs noted above, she is described as being "much taller than her native sisters" and having a body that is "beautifully proportioned, with breasts far more ample than most Japanese girls [sic]."[12] Finally, of course, neither the Japanese people broadly construed, nor their government (apart from the prime minister), seems likely to be in much sympathy with a plot of this sort, which would "risk the devastation of their nation for a cause based

---

[10]*Ibid.*, pp. 144-5, 218; 202ff., 246-9; 178-9, 491ff.
[11]*Ibid.*, pp. 537-8.
[12]*Ibid.*, pp. 140, 317-8, 140, 317. See the heroine of James Michener's 1954 bestseller, *Sayonara*, for another Japanese example of this type. The hero of that work, an American military officer, at one point offers what he considers to be a compliment to the heroine, an actress from a famous Japanese theatrical company, when he tells her "...that if she wanted to she could look almost American, ...that on a New York street few would recognize that she was from Japan" (James Michener, *Sayonara* (New York: Bantam, 1955), p. 203).

on greed by a few criminals [sic]."[13] Despite such exceptions, however, the depiction of the novel's villains clearly outweights any positive treatment of the Japanese in this work.

III. The negative depiction of Japanese culture and values

In its broader depiction of Japanese culture and values *Dragon* also utilizes a number of common stereotypes to present the Japanese in a negative light. The exclusiveness of Japanese society is given particular emphasis. "Japan is a highly honorable society. Our loyalties run very deep," Hideki Suma states at one point, to which an American replies, "Sure, to yourselves, at the expense of outsiders, such as foreign nationals."[14] On another occasion Suma explains that:

> ... Our ethics and morals come from a different breeding ground from yours. In Japan, honor and discipline are knotted tightly to loyalties-- to the Emperor, the family, and the corporation. We are not bred to venerate democratic principles or charitable generosity. The United Way, volunteer work, charity events to raise money for starving people in Africa, and organizations for providing aid to foster children in third-world countries are virtually unheard of in my country. We concentrate our benevolent efforts on taking care of our own.[15]

This exclusivity finds its greatest expression, of course, in the economic arena. "Besides being the most insular society on earth," an American character tells Suma, "Japan's problem with the rest of the world is that your business leaders have no ethics, no principles of fair play in the Western sense." The basic economic thesis put forward in the work centers on the commonly-heard complaint that the Japanese refuse to open their markets to American products, while seeking at the same time to gain complete control of the American economy, to create in effect a "new Japanese America." This includes, among other things, a Japanese plan to assume control over Hawaii and California. It is this latter idea (as well as the growing exclusivity of Japanese residential neighborhoods, resorts and golf courses in Hawaii at the present time) which prompts an American Congressman to assert, in one of the

---

[13]*Ibid.*, p. 493.
[14]*Ibid.*, p. 534.
[15]*Ibid.*, pp. 360-1.

book's more insightful moments, "...the ugly American is no more, ...[h]e's been replaced by the ugly Japanese."[16]

Japanese technological achievements are likewise depicted negatively in the novel. Robots-- one designed in the form of a vicious pursuit dog reminiscent of the Mechanical Hound in Ray Bradbury's *Fahrenheit 451*-- guard Hideki Suma's secret command center. (Fortunately, these machines are easily outwitted by American ingenuity. On one occasion the hero is able to destroy the electrical circuitry of a guard robot by using a section of hose which he has rubbed against a piece of silk.)[17] There are also Japanese projects underway to produce warships, planes and tanks controlled by robots, as well as fully automated, robot armies. Even potentially useful discoveries, such as the growth of oil-digesting microbes for cleaning up oil spills, are considered to be of equal importance for their ability "to deplete a hostile country's oil reserves."[18]

Japanese attitudes regarding the U.S. in the work are, of course, cast in a highly negative light as well. America is compared by one Japanese to "a beautiful woman who is dying of cancer," and described by another as "a land of drug addicts, Mafia gangsters, rapists and murders, homeless and illiterates." (The page following this second quote, not too surprisingly, carries a blistering counterattack from the American hero in which he makes reference, among other things, to Japan's "quaint little culture," its political corruption, and its racial prejudice.)[19]

Finally, as one might imagine in a work of this type, there are numerous references to Japanese actions during World War II. An American agent relates at one point how Japanese soldiers-- he uses the language of the wartime period and refers to them as "Nips"-- forced Allied prisoners of war in the Philippines to dig secret storage tunnels, and then buried them alive in them in order to conceal their location. This same individual provides the statistic that "fifty-seven percent of Allied soldiers in Japanese prison camps died, versus only one per cent of those held by the Germans."[20] The failure of modern day Japanese to accept responsibility for their wartime actions is also emphasized. "At least the Germans have demonstrated regret for the attrocities of the Nazis, but you people act as though your butchery of millions of

---

[16]*Ibid.*, pp. 533, 453, 473, 182, 494, 182.
[17]*Ibid.*, pp. 378, 345, 379, 401.
[18]*Ibid.*, pp. 359, 402.
[19]*Ibid.*, pp. 210, 363, 364.
[20]*Ibid.*, p. 101.

people throughout Asia and the Pacific never happened," a Congressman tells Hideki Suma. The Yasukuni Shrine controversy and the role of State Shinto during the World War II period are also mentioned.[21] In the end, the attitudes and practices of the wartime period continue to characterize and motivate contemporary Japanese behavior. Modern day *kamikaze* volunteer for suicide missions in connection with the Kaiten Project, seeing it as "an honor to give [their lives] for the new empire," and the economic demands of the plotters is likened at one point to the unconditional surrender forced on Japan at the end of the war. (When the benevolence of the U.S. Occupation is mentioned in response to these demands, the Japanese who is making them responds "bluntly"-- "I'm not here to discuss historic differences.")[22]

As in the case of its depiction of Japanese characters, not *all* of the work's treatment of contemporary Japanese culture and values is totally devoid of understanding-- there is a passage, for example, which makes at least brief mention of the country's shortage of space as a factor motivating its economic policies[23]-- still, the view it offers of Japan and its role in relation to the economic future of the U.S. in particular is, overall, a highly negative one.

IV. How should the U.S. respond?

How, in the novel's view, should the U.S. respond to the threat presented by this new, post-Cold War adversary? First of all, of course, the American people need to become aware of the problem. As one Japanese character (Ichiro Tsuboi) states in response to the economic threat: "...If we buy America it's because you're selling it." In this connection also, Americans need to know that in a very real sense they are *already* at war with Japan. Hideki Suma underlines this point, which is basically similar to that made by the authors of *The Second Pearl Harbor* (and quoted at the beginning of this essay), when he states: "We [Japanese] see no difference between an economic and a military war."[24]

Recognition of the problem should, in turn, lead to increased vigilance. The U.S. needs to allocate more money for intelligence-gathering in Japan, and to be cautious about sharing military technology. (It is asserted at one point that the Japanese have surpassed

---

[21]*Ibid.*, pp. 453, 137-8.
[22]*Ibid.*, pp. 465 (see also p. 470), 495.
[23]*Ibid.*, p. 291.
[24]*Ibid.*, pp. 183, 534.

the U.S. in Star Wars research because of the willingness of the U.S. to involve them in that project.)[25] In the economic sphere, in much the same manner discussed in Pat Choate's *Agents of Influence*, the U.S. needs to tighten its laws regarding the activities of lobbyists working for foreign governments in Washington,[26] and American politicians need to be willing to stand up on trade and economic issues (the fictional Senator Mike Diaz of New Mexico and Congresswoman Loren Smith of Colorado stand as representatives of this type in the novel). Along with this too, the U.S. needs to return to the kind of old-fashioned, American patriotism represented by the novel's hero, Dirk Pitt, of whom his boss at NUMA (the National Underwater and Marine Agency) tells another intelligence official at one point--

> ...Dirk Pitt is a bigger patriot that you and I put together. Few men have accomplished more for their country. There are few men of his breed left. He still whistles 'Yankee Doodle' in the shower and believes a handshake is a contract and a man's word is his bond. He can also be devious as the devil if he thinks he's helping preserve the Stars and Stripes, the American family, and baseball.[27]

Finally, as this quote also suggests, the U.S. needs to be ruthless in the pursuit of its goals-- following his capture at the end of the novel, Hideki Suma is kept in a semi-drugged state until he has been thoroughly debriefed, at which point, according to an American agent, "a little something extra [will be slipped] into his noodle soup."[28]

If all of this carries with it a mood of paranoia and an assertion of the need for eternal vigilance reminiscent of the earlier Cold War relationship between the U.S. and the Soviet Union-- even the hero wonders at one point whether there might not be bombs hidden under the floor of the restaurant where he is eating[29]-- the answer is clearly: *yes.* The dust jacket of the hardcover edition of the novel captures the mood of the work nicely when it states that the author "mixes recent history with some of our deepest fears." Clearly Japan is well on its way here to becoming the new, post-Cold War adversary of the U.S., functioning even as a means of tightening the bond between the U.S. and the, at that time still-existing, Soviet Union. In this connection, as

---

[25]*Ibid.*, pp. 109, 177.
[26]*Ibid.*, p. 419.
[27]*Ibid.*, p. 163.
[28]*Ibid.*, p. 535.
[29]*Ibid.*, p. 166.

one intelligence officer puts it: "We're all in the same boat now, both threatened by another superpower."[30]

V. A footnote on Michael Crichton's *Rising Sun*

Since the publication of *Dragon*, the popular culture scene in the U.S. has, of course, seen the publication of the even more successful fictional bestseller dealing with Japan and the Japanese, Michael Crichton's *Rising Sun* (1992). Because it deals with many of the same themes as the earlier book, some brief discussion of Crichton's work is of interest here.

While *Dragon*, for all of its discussion of economic themes, remains primarily a post-Cold War adventure story which happens to use the Japanese and a set of stereotypes concerning them as a replacement for the Soviets as its principal villains,[31] *Rising Sun* involves a much more directed effort at sensitizing its readers to 'the Japanese threat.' Scarcely less preposterous in plot-- in *Rising Sun* a young American woman is found murdered at the grand opening of a Japanese office building in Los Angeles and as the story proceeds a plot to use the event to bribe a U.S. senator is uncovered-- it is nevertheless told with considerably more sophistication and believability. Along with a full cast of Japanese villains, including the plot's chief planner (and actual murderer) who is disavowed by his superiors at the end and commits suicide,[32] there are also a large number of Americans from a variety of business, journalistic and technological backgrounds who come forward during the course of the story and speak with the knowledge of experts concerning the Japanese threat and the American mistakes that have contributed to it.[33] As in the earlier novel, numerous racial and cultural stereotypes are employed. (Among the stereotypes

---

[30]*Ibid.*, p. 192.

[31]Cussler's most recent work, *Sahara* (1992), uses "a ruthless West African dictator and [a] French industialist" (cover of paperback edition - London: Grafton, 1993) as the villains.

[32]Michael Crichton, *Rising Sun* (London: Arrow, 1992), pp. 386-390.

[33]Among the most significant of these are: Dr. Phillip Sanders, a physics professor who discourses on the state of American higher education (pp. 208ff.), Jenny Gonzales, a lab technician who discusses the state of Japanese video technology vis-a-vis that of the U.S. (see especially p. 104), and a journalist, Ron Levine, who discusses Japanese trade practices and a number of related subjects (pp. 234ff.).

depicted in the book are: Japanese moral relativism and ruthlessness in
the pursuit of their ends, the exclusivity of Japanese society, Japanese
racial prejudices, and even a supposed Japanese predeliction for kinky
sex.[34]) As in the earlier work also, economic concerns lie at the heart of
the message. A "Japanese motto," "Business is war," serves as one of
the work's epigraphs, and the book's non-fiction "Afterword" (in which
the author restates his thesis, complete with a bibliography of non-
fictional sources on the subject, for anyone who may have missed the
point during the course of the story) is headed by a well-known
quotation from Japanese business leader Akio Morita, "If you don't
want Japan to buy it, don't sell it."[35] Finally, a mood of paranoia
similar to that found in *Dragon* also prevails. (One of the book's more
subtle and yet frightening moments depicts a seminar for American
employees of Japanese companies-- a glimpse of a totally Japan-
dominated U.S. economy of the future?-- where the chief theme is "You
will succeed if you remember *to know your place*," and even the
existence of bars and restaurants in U.S. cities which cater to a Japanese
clientele are described in the novel as a kind of darkly threatening
"shadow world."[36]) Although the book occasionally displays a respect
for certain aspects of Japanese   culture-- one of the main characters, a
police captain named John Connor who has spent a considerable
amount of time in Japan, serves as the chief spokesperson for this point
of view[37]-- and at some junctures seems as critical of the U.S. as it is of

---

[34]*Ibid.*, pp. 67-8; 163; 380-1; 79. One theme that is given significantly
less emphasis in this work than in *Dragon* is the Japanese role in World War
II. Although the reader learns during the course of the story that one
character's particular dislike of the Japanese can be attributed to the fact that
his uncle died under mysterious circumstances as a Japanese war prisoner,
the comment is also made that war memories should be put aside-- "It's a
different country now." (p. 145).

[35]*Ibid.*, pp. [8], [400].

[36]*Ibid.*, pp. 196 (emphasis in the original), 71. In a similar vein there are
numerous examples of Japanese in high places exerting influence to impede
the police investigation of the murder (see pp. 85, 181, 185), and, as
evidence as well of the level of 'literary art' employed in *Rising Sun*, the
author intersperses material regarding the evil witch in Walt Disney's
Sleeping Beauty, playing on a VCR in the background, as a means of
heightening the dramatic tension as Japanese thugs move in on the hero's
house in the attempt to kill him (pp. 362, 366, 368).

[37]See pp. 380-1 for a final summation of this character's basically
ambivalent attitude regarding Japan.

Japan,[38] the overall tone of the novel, as in Cussler's earlier work, involves a highly negative portrayal of its subject. The question of the respective audiences for the two books is, of course, also a matter of interest here. Given its author's reputation and the fact that *Rising Sun* was widely reviewed-- including a largely favorable front page review in the prestigious *New York Times Book Review*[39] (Cussler's works tend not to be reviewed in such places)-- argues for a better educated and more intellectually-attuned readership for Crichton's work. Still, in the final analysis both works in plot and treatment fall clearly into the domain of popular as opposed to serious fiction, and serve to mark the trend toward the increasingly negative treatment of Japan in this form of popular culture.

VI. The significance of these works

What is the larger significance of works like *Dragon* and *Rising Sun* in determining contemporary American attitudes regarding Japan? As we are all too aware, popular culture in the modern world is an extremely pervasive phenomena. More people read bestsellers or watch television movies depicting controversial issues than read balanced accounts or attend academic lectures on these subjects. For this reason most people's opinions on such matters are heavily influenced by the treatments in popular culture they are exposed to. Popular fiction, along with other forms of fictionalized portrayals in films and television, carry an added dimension as well. While someone who reads a popular *non*-fiction account of a subject (or views a television special report concerning it) probably has at least some degree of prior interest in the subject and is making a conscious choice to read or view the work in question, the individual who picks a bestselling novel off of an airport or supermarket display rack (or flips on a made-for-television movie) is more than likely looking simply for entertainment. When such an individual in search of an action/adventure story or a murder mystery inadvertently selects a *Dragon* or a *Rising Sun* they are in fact receiving a largely unanticipated but highly-effective indoctrination into a set of negative values and stereotypes regarding Japan. The fact that this seems to be occurring with increasing frequency in connection with books of this type dealing with Japan should be a matter of concern for

---

[38]Crichton uses the image of a "drunken uncle" (p. 126) to portray the current state of the U.S., softening slightly Cussler's image of "a beautiful woman dying of cancer" (see footnote 19 above).
[39]February 9, 1992.

all serious-minded individuals interested in maintaining a positive relationship between our two countries. In the long run, the process of overcoming differences between nations, be they economic or otherwise, is seldom facilitated by the creation of stereotypes or paranoia concerning the other country's people and culture.[40]

---

[40]Fortunately, this negative direction in popular fiction is offset by a somewhat more positive depiction of Japan in other forms of contemporary popular entertainment. One thinks for example of recent popular films such as *Gung Ho* or *Mr. Baseball* which deal with differences between the U.S. and Japan in a more comic and light-hearted manner. Similarly, advance reports regarding the film adaptation of *Rising Sun* (due for release in July of 1993) seem to indicate a significant lessening of the anti-Japanese theme in that work, although Asian-American civil rights groups in the U.S. were demonstrating against it at the time that this article went to press.

List of Works Consulted

Andrew Adams & Mark Schilling, *Jesse! Sumo Superstar* (The Japan Times: 1985).

Pat Barr, *The Deer Cry Pavilion; A Story of Westerners in Japan 1868-1905* (Penguin: 1988).

Ruth Benedict, *The Chrysanthemum and the Sword; Patterns of Japanese Culture* (Houghton Mifflin: 1989).

Isabella L. Bird, *Unbeaten Tracks in Japan* (Beacon: 1987).

Margaret M. Caffrey, *Ruth Benedict: Stranger in This Land* (University of Texas: 1989).

Pat Choate, *Agents of Influence* (Knopf: 1990).

Jonathan Cott, *Wandering Ghost: The Odyssey of Lafcadio Hearn* (Kodansha: 1992).

Michael Crichton, *Rising Sun* (Arrow: 1992).

Current Biography (H.W.Wilson: 1941--).

Clive Cussler, *Dragon* (Simon and Schuster: 1991).

Carl Dawson, *Lafcadio Hearn and the Vision of Japan* (Johns Hopkins University: 1992).

A. Grove Day, *James A. Michener* (Twayne: 1964).

John W. Dower, *Japan in War and Peace: Selected Essays* (New Press: 1993).

Encyclopedia Americana (Grolier: 1990).

Herbert Feis, *The Road to Pearl Harbor; The Coming of the War Between the United States and Japan* (Princeton University: 1971).

"Frank Lloyd Wright and Japan," *Frank Lloyd Wright Quarterly*, Vol. 6, No. 2 (Spring 1995), pp. 3-7.

Great Historical Figures of Japan (Japan Culture Institute: 1978).

Joseph C. Grew, *Ten Years in Japan* (Simon and Schuster: 1944).

John Whitney Hall, *Japan: From Prehistory to Modern Times* (Tuttle: 1971).

Mikiso Hane, *Modern Japan: A Historical Survey* (Westview: 1986).

Lafcadio Hearn, *Glimpses of Unfamiliar Japan* (Tuttle: 1976).

_____ , *Japan: An Attempt at Interpretation* (Tuttle: 1955).

William J. Higginson with Penny Harter, *The Haiku Handbook; How to Write, Share, and Teach Haiku* (Kodansha: 1989).

Francis L. K. Hsu, *Psychological Anthropology* (Dorsey: 1961).

International Encyclopedia of the Social Sciences (Crowell Collier & Macmillan: 1968).

Cary James, *Frank Lloyd Wright's Imperial Hotel* (Dover: 1968).

Sheila K. Johnson, *The Japanese Through American Eyes* (Stanford University: 1988).

William H. Jordy, *American Buildings and Their Architects - Vol. 5: The Impact of European Modernism in the Mid-Twentieth Century* (Oxford University: 1972).

Donald Keene, *Appreciations of Japanese Culture* (Kodansha: 1981).

_____ , *Japanese Literature; An Introduction for Western Readers* (Tuttle: 1977).

Jack Kerouac, *The Dharma Bums* (Penguin: 1976).

Kodansha Encyclopedia of Japan (Kodansha: 1983).

Clay Lancaster, *The Japanese Influence in America* (Abbeville Press: 1983).

Jon Livingston, Joe Moore & Felicia Oldfather, eds., *Postwar Japan, 1945 to the Present* (Pantheon: 1973).

William Manchester, *American Caesar; Douglas MacArthur, 1880-1964* (Little, Brown: 1978).

R.H.P. Mason & J.G. Caiger, *A History of Japan* (Tuttle: 1973).

Margaret Mead, *An Anthropologist at Work; Writings of Ruth Benedict* (Greenwood Press: 1977).

_____, *Ruth Benedict* (Columbia University: 1974).

James A. Michener, *The Bridges at Toko-ri* (Fawcett: 1953).

_____, *Sayonara* (Bantam: 1955).

_____, *The Voice of Asia* (Random House: 1951).

Richard H. Minear, "The Wartime Studies of Japanese National Character," *The Japan Interpreter*, Vol. 13, No. 1 (Summer 1980), pp. 36-59.

Judith Schachter Modell, *Ruth Benedict; Pattern of a Life* (University of Pennsylvania: 1983).

Hyoe Murakami, *Japan: The Years of Trial, 1919-52* (Kodansha: 1983).

Lady Murasaki, *The Tale of Genji*, transl. by Arthur Waley (Doubleday: 1955).

Murasaki Shikibu, *The Tale of Genji*, transl. by Edward G. Seidensticker, Vol. 1 (Tuttle: 1978).

Corinne J. Naden, *Frank Lloyd Wright: The Rebel Architect* (Franklin Watts: 1968).

The New Encyclopaedia Britannica (University of Chicago: 1990).

The New Official Guide: Japan (Japan National Tourist Organization: 1975).

Dorothy Perkins, *The Encyclopedia of Japan* (Facts on File: 1991).

T. Boone Pickens et al., *The Second Pearl harbor* (National Press: 1991).

William J. Puette, *Guide to The Tale of Genji by Murasaki Shikibu* (Tuttle: 1983).

Edwin O. Reischauer, *Japan: The Story of a Nation*, 4th ed. (? : 1990).

_____, *My Life Between Japan and America* (Harper & Row: 1986).

Haru Matsukata Reischauer, *Samurai and Silk; A Japanese and American Heritage* (Tuttle: 1987).

J. Thomas Rimer, *A Reader's Guide to Japanese Literature* (Kodansha: 1988).

G.B. Sansom, *A History of Japan, 1615-1867* (Tuttle: 1974)

_____, *A History of Japan, 1334-1615* (Tuttle: 1974).

_____, *The Western World and Japan: A Study in the Interaction of European and Asiatic Cultures* (Tuttle: 1977).

Michael Schaller, *Douglas MacArthur: The Far Eastern General* (Oxford University: 1989).

Conrad Schirokauer, *A Brief History of Japanese Civilization* (Harcourt Brace Jovanovich: 1993).

Meryle Secrest, *Frank Lloyd Wright* (Knopf: 1992).

Edward G. Seidensticker, "Introduction" to Murasaki Shikibu, *The Tale of Genji*, transl. by Edward G. Seidensticker, Vol. 1 (Tuttle: 1978), pp. vii-xv.

Michael Shapiro, *Japan: In the Land of the Brokenhearted* (Holt: 1989).

Lora Sharnoff, *Grand Sumo; The Living Sport and Tradition*, Revised edition (Weatherhill: 1993).

Oliver Statler, *Shimoda Story* (Tuttle: 1971)

Richard Storry, *A History of Modern Japan* (Penguin: 1982).

Richard Tames, *Servant of the Shogun; Being the True Story of William Adams, Pilot and Samurai, The First Englishman in Japan* (Paul Norbury: 1981).

Masami Tanigawa, "Wright's Little-Known Japanese Projects," *Frank Lloyd Wright Quarterly*, Vol. 6, No. 2 (Spring 1995), pp.16-20.

Sheridan M. Tatsuno, *Created in Japan: From Imitators to World-Class Innovators* (Harper & Row: 1990).

George Brown Tindall, *America: A Narrative History*, 2nd ed., Vol. 2 (Norton: 1988).

John Tran, "So Wrong Frank Lloyd Wright," *Kansai Time Out*, August 1993, p. 12.

Robert Whiting, *The Chrysanthemum and the Bat; The Game Japanese Play* (The Permanent Press: 1977).

Harold S. Williams, *Foreigners in Mikadoland* (Tuttle: 1963).

_____, *Shades of the Past, or Indiscreet Tales of Japan* (Tuttle: 1958).

Harry Wray & Hilary Conroy, eds., *Japan Examined; Perspectives on Modern Japanese History* (University of Hawaii: 1983).

Frank Lloyd Wright, *An Autobiography* (Horizon Press: 1977); also 1932 edition of the same, in *Frank Lloyd Wright Collected Writings*, Vol. 2 (Rizzoli: 1992).

Scott Wright teaches history at the University of St. Thomas in St. Paul, Minnesota. He has spent a total of four years living and working in Japan since receiving a Fulbright teaching grant there in 1979. He is the author (with Teruo Motomura) of *A Short History of the United States* (1988; published in Japan) and a novel, *The Lynching of John Hanson*, in 1986.